MATTHEW

The Beginning of Sorrows

MATTHEW

The Beginning of Sorrows

By
Salem Kirban

MOODY PRESS
CHICAGO

MOODY PRESS EDITION, 1972

Library of Congress Catalog Card No.: 72-79800
ISBN: 0-8024-5211-6

ACKNOWLEDGMENTS

To **Dr. Gary G.** **Cohen,** professor of Greek and New Testament at Biblical School
of Theology, Hatfield, Pennsylvania, who carefully checked the final manuscript
and supplied the proper color coding for each verse.

To **Edston Detrich,** artist, who skillfully designed the front cover.

To **Doreen Kirban** and **Wesley Frick,** who devoted many long hours to proofreading
the text again and again, and again.

To the many photographers throughout the world who pooled their resources so
that we might have exclusive photographs that accurately depict these Last Days,
including Wide World Photos, Helmut K. Wimmer, Dr. Landrum B. Shettles, Black
Star, Magnum, NASA, New York Times, Compix, Culver Pictures, Bettman Archive,
LIFE, Joel Gower, and Gamma.

King James scripture text is from the New Scofield Reference Bible. Copyright
© 1967 by Oxford University Press, Inc. Used with permission.

DEDICATION

To my wife, Mary. Her life is a constant inspiration to me.

HERE ARE THE EXCLUSIVE FEATURES OF The BEGINNING OF SORROWS and Kirban's PROPHECY NEW TESTAMENT

(KING JAMES VERSION)

THE BEGINNING OF SORROWS (Matthew) is the *first* book in our PROPHECY NEW TESTAMENT series. It will give you an insight into the visual format of Kirban's PROPHECY NEW TESTAMENT. Kirban's PROPHECY NEW TESTAMENT includes REVELATION VISUALIZED. This custom combination gives a most complete NEW TESTAMENT whose emphasis is on the prophetic promises and judgments of God.

Combining the Prophecy New Testament with Revelation Visualized will make available to you a compact set of books of over 1500-pages. Current, up-to-date photographs and charts give added clarity to prophetic portions of Scripture . . . helps clear away clouds of doubt.

COLOR KEYED VERSES MAKE PROPHECY COME ALIVE

Identification by COLOR makes it easy to determine prophetic TIME PERIOD. Dr. Gary G. Cohen, Professor of New Testament at Biblical School of Theology, Hatfield, Pennsylvania, served as Consultant in selecting prophetic verses and determining color arrangement.

Prophecies fulfilled in the PAST are marked in BROWN.
BROWN is representative of the color of the ancient SOILS uncovered by archeologists.

Prophecies to be fulfilled in the Last 3 1/2 years of the TRIBULATION are marked in RED.
RED is representative of BLOOD and the awesome judgments.

Prophecies being fulfilled today (PRESENT) are marked in GRAY.
GRAY represents the color of a TRANSITION period before the great events of the Second Coming of the Lord.

Prophecies to be fulfilled during the time period of the battle of ARMAGEDDON are marked in GREEN.
GREEN is used to represent God's JEALOUS wrath.

Prophecies that will occur at the time of the RAPTURE are marked in YELLOW.
YELLOW is representative of the CROWN REWARDS.

Prophecies to be fulfilled in the MILLENNIUM are marked in BLUE.
BLUE is often identified with the HEAVENLY Kingdom on earth.

Prophecies to be fulfilled in the First 3 1/2 years of the TRIBULATION are marked in ORANGE, indicative of FIRE. Tells us of approaching, more drastic judgments.

Prophecies to be fulfilled when the NEW HEAVENS & NEW EARTH are formed are marked in PURPLE.
PURPLE is representative of ROYALTY.

WHY Kirban's
PROPHECY NEW TESTAMENT Series WAS CREATED

THE BEGINNING OF SORROWS *(Matthew)* is the first book in our
Prophecy New Testament Series. It is an excellent example of the
"visualized," easy-to-understand format that is followed in the entire
series — Matthew through Revelation.

Because far too many have not made a searching study of the Scriptures they come up with misconceptions about God's Plan for tomorrow
in the light of Bible prophecy. In some ways it compares to man's ideas
about the universe.

Ancient man as well as modern man have devised elaborate expla-
nations for the observable universe.

For example, the ancient Egyptians considered their world to be a
large, rectangular box (illustrated above). The larger dimension of the
rectangle was from north to south; the shorter, from east to west. The
bottom of the box was the earth, where continents and seas alternated.
Egypt was at the center of the narrow, sunken floor, and at the top of
the box was the sky.

The sky was supported by mountain peaks, which were joined together
by rolling hills, creating a wall that surround the world. To the
Egyptians, the near surface of the sky, the part toward the earth, is
hung with lamps held securely by strong ropes. The sun is a disk of
fire, the god Ra, which floats in a barge on the celestial river. At sun-
set the boat passes into the valley of the gods.

To the Chaldeans, the universe was a completely enclosed region that
floated on top of the great sea. The sea between the central earth and
the surrounding wall was completely forbidden. A person would be lost
6   forever if he ventured upon it.

The ancient Greeks believed that the earth was flat.

To the Hindus the bottom of the universe was a sea of milk bounding on all sides. A huge turtle swam in the sea, and became the foundation for the world. Four elephants stood on the turtle's back at each of the four cardinal points: north, east, south, and west.

Today as you and I read these misconceptions about the universe... they seem absurd. And, of course, they are.

Man today realizes that these are gross misconceptions, because U.S. spacemen have traveled to the moon and we have seen both our earth and the moon in their proper perspective. As man's scientific achievements becomes more highly refined, his data becomes more accurate.

Yet, in spite of our scientific, medical, industrial and educational advances the spiritual climate of the world appears to be hitting new lows. *There is no other event yet to take place prior to the Second Coming of Jesus Christ* (the Rapture). And this paradox (scientific advance and moral decline) may be the stepping stone to the ushering in of Antichrist. It can well be that this generation, right now, will witness the RAPTURE!

Time is so short...and yet how many people still have misconceptions about God's Plan for the ages. How many people are really aware of what God reveals in the Bible concerning this life, life after death, hell, judgment, eternal life and heaven!

Although man may be intellectually and scientifically advanced much of his "religious" thinking is formulated on either (a) what his parents taught him or (b) what he personally wishes to believe God would or would not do.

How many times have you heard the remark, "A loving God would not send anyone to Hell," or "I've lived a good life, I've earned a place in Heaven."

To many, perhaps even you, your spiritual experience is equal, in parallel, to the ancient Egyptian concept of the universe...based on myth and theory.

It is my hope that THE BEGINNING OF SORROWS (Matthew) will reveal to you how much of the New Testament deals with future events to come...**your future.** And that being so challenged and stimulated, you will secure the complete edition of Kirban's PROPHECY NEW TESTAMENT which includes the books of MATTHEW through REVELATION. There are more than 300 Old and New Testament Scriptures which promise that Jesus Christ will return to earth!

And these promises will be fulfilled just as literally as the 200 Old Testament prophecies of His virgin birth, death, burial and resurrection were fulfilled in His first coming when He suffered and died for man's sins.

The special color coding, the hundreds of photographs of today's events, should reveal to you more than ever before that we are living in the LAST DAYS just prior to the Rapture. In light of this, *what are you doing about it?*

Salem Kirban

PROPHECY RAPIDLY HEADING FOR FULFILLMENT IN HOLY LAND

The turning point was June, 1967.

Not since Solomon's kingdom of Jerusalem in the 10th Century B.C. has Israel's realm been so vast and powerful. In 1971 the Israelis control 26,500 square miles of former Arab territory.

How much territory the Israelis will give back...no one knows. One Israeli perhaps prophetically stated, "You can tell which areas we intend to keep by the amount of money we're putting into them."

Israeli leaders are sure of one thing. They will never agree to let Jerusalem be a divided city again. Since 1969 the Israelis have been developing a Master Plan for Metropolitan Jerusalem which envisages, in the year 2010, a population of 890,000, of whom 465,000 would be Jews (Present 1971 population of Jerusalem is 290,000, of which 225,000 are Jews). Within 5 years, however, Jeru-

salem as we now know it may become a "lost" city. Already 2600 housing units are being built and long range plans call for the construction of a total of 25,000 units to house over 100,000 more Israelis.

The Housing ministry is now developing an enormous residential area for 50,000 persons on the empty Judean hills. Look at the photograph above. If it seems hazy to you, IT IS! The haze is created by a cloud of smoke you can see every day. It comes from a quarry in the Jerusalem area...adding immensely to the pollution over the Jerusalem valley.

One of the architects invited to a special conference to discuss the Master Plan for Jerusalem suggested the Jerusalem be granted extra-territorial status so that it could become a "world city" rather than a national capital.

Look for the skyline of Jerusalem to change. With modernization Jerusalem may well become a world city. Traditional sites precious to Christians may soon be surrounded by tall buildings and multi-lane highways. Watch for further developments in Jerusalem. They may well be a barometer of the End Times!

Teddy Kollek, the mayor of Jerusalem, inspects building plans with an associate. These blueprints are part of the Master Plan for the New Jerusalem that will make this sacred spot a "city of the world."

The Gospel according to MATTHEW

THE AUTHOR	Matthew
WHERE WRITTEN	Possibly at Antioch in Syria
WHEN	c. A.D. 50
TO WHOM	Principally for readers familiar with the Old Testament prophecies—hence **to Jews**
THEME	Christ as Messiah and King

BACKGROUND

Matthew was probably not the first book of the New Testament to be written, even though it is placed first in its present order today.

Matthew was a tax collector. He was a Jew who collected taxes for the Roman government. Because of this, loyal Jews had no love for him. Little is known of him except his name and occupation. While he was stationed at Capernaum (where he collected taxes), Jesus called him to be one of His disciples (Matthew 9:9).

Luke and Mark give his name as Levi. In the eyes of many of the Jews it was unusual for Jesus to call Matthew as an apostle since his despised occupation ceremonially made him an outcast. This selection by Jesus showed that His ministry was independent of the organized religion of His time.

There is at least one vital difference between Matthew and the other three Gospels. It is this. Matthew makes more references to Old Testament writings than do the others. His aim is to show that Jesus was the promised Messiah whose coming was foretold by the Old Testament prophets.

In chapters 5-7 Matthew includes the most complete text of the Sermon on the Mount. It is also interesting to note that the following incidents appear only in Matthew:

(1:20-24)	The vision of Joseph
(2:1-12)	The visit of the Magi
(2:13-15)	The flight into Egypt
(2:16)	The massacre of the infants
(27:19)	The dream of Pilate's wife
(27:3-10)	The death of Judas
(27:52)	The resurrection of the saints at the crucifixion
(28:12-15)	The bribery of the guard
(28:19-20)	The baptismal commission

Matthew's Gospel is intended for instruction (didactic). It contains the largest single block of instructional material found in the Gospels. And these discourses comprise about three-fifths of the entire Gospel.

You will find that Matthew is the only Gospel in which the word "church" occurs. See Matthew 16:18 and 18:17.

As Merrill C. Tenney so aptly stated it, "Matthew is the Gospel of the King." It thus gives details on the royal genealogy through the line of King David and on the birth of Jesus.

Declarations of Israel's coming trials appear chiefly in Matthew, as do most of Jesus' remarks on the End Times.

THE GOSPEL ACCORDING TO

MATTHEW

CHAPTER 1

Genealogy
c. 5 B.C.

1 1 The book of the genealogy of Jesus Christ, the son of David, the son of Abraham.

2 Abraham begot Isaac; and Isaac begot Jacob; and Jacob begot Judah and his brethren;

3 And Judah begot Perez and Zerah of Tamar; and Perez begot Hezron; and Hezron begot Ram;

4 And Ram begot Amminadab; and Amminadab begot Nahshon; and Nahshon begot Salmon;

5 And Salmon begot Boaz of Rahab; and Boaz begot Obed of Ruth; and Obed begot Jesse;

6 And Jesse begot David, the king; and David, the king, begot Solomon of her *that had been the wife* of Uriah;

7 And Solomon begot Rehoboam; and Rehoboam begot Abijah; and Abijah begot Asa;

8 And Asa begot Jehoshaphat; and Jehoshaphat begot Joram; and Joram begot Uzziah;

9 And Uzziah begot Jotham; and Jotham begot Ahaz; and Ahaz begot Hezekiah;

10 And Hezekiah begot Manasseh; and Manasseh begot Amon; and Amon begot Josiah;

11 And Josiah begot Jeconiah and his brethren, about the time they were carried away to Babylon.

12 And after they were brought to Babylon, Jeconiah begot Shealtiel; and Shealtiel begot Zerubbabel;

13 And Zerubbabel begot Abiud; and Abiud begot Eliakim; and Eliakim begot Azor;

14 And Azor begot Sadoc; and Sadoc begot Achim; and Achim begot Eliud;

15 And Eliud begot Eleazar; and Eleazar begot Matthan; and Matthan begot Jacob;

16 And Jacob begot Joseph, the husband of Mary, of whom was born Jesus, who is called Christ.

17 So all the generations from Abraham to David *are* fourteen generations; and from David until the carrying away into Babylon *are* fourteen generations; and from the carrying away into Babylon unto Christ *are* fourteen generations.

Announcement to Joseph of Jesus' Birth
• *Nazareth*
Isaiah 9:67

18 Now the birth of Jesus Christ was in this way: When as His mother, Mary, was espoused to Joseph, before they came together, she was found with child of the Holy Spirit.

1 (1:1) Messiah (Christ) was to be of the lineage of Abraham and David. Isaiah 11:1,9; Jeremiah 33:15; Genesis 22:15-18.

(Matthew 1:1)
GENEALOGIES EXPLAINED

The Church of Jesus Christ of Latter-day Saints (Mormons) has accumulated the largest public genealogical library in the world.

They, in error, believe that by keeping records of their ancestral line and baptizing for their dead relatives, salvation for their departed ones will be assured. THIS IS NOT SCRIPTURAL! Yet in a mountain near Salt Lake City they have six huge vault storage rooms capable of holding 25 million microfilmed 300-page volumes of genealogies! Genealogies are a record of one's ancestry.

The New Testament contains two genealogies of our Lord. The first is found here in Matthew 1... the other in Luke 3:23-38.

Matthew's gospel was written with Jewish readers in mind and therefore his genealogy begins with Abraham. It ends with Joseph, husband of Mary. In Luke we find the genealogy beginning with Joseph and tracing it all the way back to Adam. Since Luke wrote for the Greek world, he traces the genealogy back to the fountainhead of the entire race, Adam.

The careful examiner of the two genealogies will find that the two genealogies take different routes from David, the King, to Joseph. The Matthew genealogy goes from:
David to Solomon... and finally to... Jacob begetting Joseph.
The Luke genealogy goes from:
David to Nathan (one of his sons)... and finally to... Heli and then to Joseph.

On *Heli,* the identification by Godet, that great scholar of yesteryear, seems to have the most merit, namely that Heli is: The father of Mary, and the brother of Jacob the father of Joseph.

Accordingly then we have the routes of the genealogies as follows:

Matthew:		*Luke:*
		Adam
Abraham		Abraham
David		David
Solomon ←——— *Both Sons of David* ———→		Nathan
Matthan ←——— *Same Man* ———→		Mathat
Jacob [Father of Joseph] ←— *Brothers* ——→		Heli [Father of Mary]
Joseph		Joseph
Jesus		Jesus

Luke shows that Christ is the royal Messianic *bloodline* by Mary. Matthew shows that Joseph, the adopted father of Jesus, was also of the royal line— hence, Joseph's *legal* son, Jesus, was *lawfully* of the royal line. That two routes in the genealogists are possible will be of no surprise to anyone familiar with the intermarrying which occurs among families which for generations live near one another.

(Matthew 1:1)

Interior of Granite Mountain Records Vault. Presently the Mormons have microfilmed genealogical records which represent 2½ million printed volumes of 300 pages each!

19 Then Joseph, her husband, being a just *man,* and not willing to make her a public example, was minded to put her away privately.

20 But while he thought on these things, behold, an angel of the Lord appeared unto him in a dream, saying, Joseph, thou son of David, fear not to take unto thee Mary, thy wife; for that which is conceived in her is of the Holy Spirit.

21 And she shall bring forth a son, and thou shalt call His name JESUS; for He shall save His people from their sins.

1 22 Now all this was done, that it might be fulfilled which was spoken by the Lord through the prophet, saying,

23 Behold, the virgin shall be with child, and shall bring forth a son, and they shall call His name Immanuel, which, being interpreted, is God with us.

Birth of Christ
● *Bethlehem*
Luke 2:1-7, Isaiah 7:14

24 Then Joseph, being raised from sleep, did as the angel of the Lord had bidden him, and took unto him his wife,

25 And knew her not till she had brought forth her first-born son; and he called His name JESUS.

CHAPTER 2

Visit of the Wise Men
c. 4 B.C.
● *Jerusalem and Bethlehem*
Numbers 24:17

2 1 Now when Jesus was born in Bethlehem of Judaea in the days of Herod, the king, behold, there came wise men from the east to Jerusalem,

2 Saying, Where is He that is born King of the Jews? For we have seen His star in the east, and are come to worship Him.

3 When Herod, the king, had heard *these things,* he was troubled, and all Jerusalem with him.

4 And when he had gathered all the chief priests and scribes of the people together, he demanded of them where the Christ should be born.

5 And they said unto him, In Bethlehem of Judaea; for thus it is written by the prophet,

6 And thou Bethlehem, *in* the land of Judah, art not the least among the princes of Judah; for out of thee shall come a Governor that shall rule My people, Israel.

7 Then Herod, when he had privately called the wise men, inquired of them diligently what time the star appeared.

8 And he sent them to Bethlehem, and said, Go and search diligently for the young child; and when ye have found *Him,* bring me word again, that I may come and worship Him also.

9 When they had heard the king, they departed; and, lo, the star, which they saw in the east, went before them, till it came and stood over where the young child was.

10 When they saw the star, they rejoiced with exceedingly great joy.

11 And when they were come into the house, they saw the young child with Mary, His mother, and fell down, and worshiped Him; and when they had opened their treasures, they presented unto Him gifts: gold, and frankincense, and myrrh.

12 And being warned of God in a dream that they should not return to Herod, they departed into their own country another way.

---

1 (1:22-23) Therefore the Lord Himself shall give you a sign; Behold, the virgin shall conceive, and bear a son, and shall call His name Immanuel (Isaiah 7:14).

2 (2:1, 5-6) But thou, Bethlehem Ephratah, though thou be little among the thousands of Judah, yet out of thee shall He come forth unto Me that is to be ruler in Israel; whose goings forth have been from of old, from everlasting (Micah 5:2).

PAST	PRESENT	RAPTURE	FIRST 3½ LAST 3½ TRIBULATION	ARMA-GEDDON	MIL-LENNIUM	NEW HEAVENS & EARTH

(Matthew 2:9)

This photograph was taken in Bethlehem at the Shepherd's field and, overlooks the possible route taken by the Magi, known as "wise men." See Matthew 2:1-12. In those days "wise men" were those who were experts in many arts including the study of stars. The suggestion by some that these magi were merely astrologers is an hypothesis which has never been proven.

Contrary to popular belief, nothing in Scripture suggests that there were 3 wise men or that they were kings.

● *Bethlehem,*
Jerusalem and Egypt

13 And when they were departed, behold, an angel of the Lord appeareth to Joseph in a dream, saying, Arise, and take the young child and His mother, and flee into Egypt, and be thou there until I bring thee word; for Herod will seek the young child to destroy Him.

14 When he arose, he took the young child and His mother by night, and departed into Egypt:

Flight to Egypt and
Slaughter of Innocents
Jeremiah 31:15

1 15 And was there until the death of Herod, that it might be fulfilled which was spoken by the Lord through the prophet, saying, Out of Egypt have I called My son.

16 Then Herod, when he saw that he was mocked of the wise men, was exceedingly angry, and sent forth, and slew all the children that were in Bethlehem, and in all its borders, from two years old and under, according to the time which he had diligently inquired of the wise men.

2 17 Then was fulfilled that which was spoken by Jeremiah, the prophet, saying,

18 In Ramah was there a voice heard, lamentation, and weeping, and great mourning, Rachel weeping for her children, and would not be comforted, because they are not.

From Egypt to Nazareth
with Jesus
c. 4 B.C. or 3 B.C.
Luke 2:39

19 But when Herod was dead, behold, an angel of the Lord appeareth in a dream to Joseph in Egypt,

20 Saying, Arise, and take the young child and His mother, and go into the land of Israel; for they are dead who sought the young child's life.

21 And he arose, and took the young child and His mother, and came into the land of Israel.

22 But when he heard that Archelaus did reign in Judaea in the place of his father, Herod, he was afraid to go there; notwithstanding, being warned of God in a dream, he turned aside into the parts of Galilee;

23 And he came and dwelt in a city 3 called Nazareth, that it might be fulfilled which was spoken by the prophets, He shall be called a Nazarene.

CHAPTER 3

John's Ministry Begins
26 A.D.
● *Judean Wilderness*
Mark 1:1, Luke 3:1-2,
John 1:19-28, Malachi 3:1

1 In those days came John the Baptist, preaching in the wilderness of Judaea,

1 (2:15) Hosea 11:1. Matthew, through the Spirit of God, beholds this verse of Hosea which primarily speaks of the nation Israel coming out of Egypt. Here the nation was nurtured in Egypt until its maturity as a son. Matthew sees this as a type of Christ's being summoned from Egypt when He too was a child. Here the Old Testament prophecy was "fulfilled" in the sense of "additionally filled."

2 (2:17-18) Thus saith the Lord; A voice was heard in Ramah, lamentation, and bitter weeping; Rachel weeping for her children, refused to be comforted for her children, because they were not (Jeremiah 31:15).

3 (2:23) Messiah was to be the "Branch" of Isaiah 11:1. "Branch" in Hebrew is *Nazar.*

PAST	PRESENT	RAPTURE	FIRST 3½ LAST 3½ TRIBULATION	ARMA-GEDDON	MIL-LENNIUM	NEW HEAVENS & EARTH

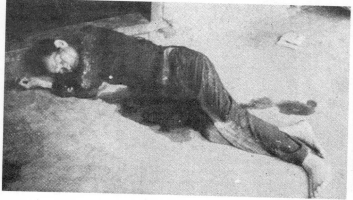

(Matthew 2:16)

MASSACRES AS CURRENT AS TODAY

In March, 1968 inexperienced GI's prepared to assault My Lai, a village in South Vietnam. The central platoon of about 30 men entered but met no resistance.

But in less than 20 minutes they burned the village, chased the villagers into groups and mercilessly killed everyone...elderly men, women and children. Over 100 died.

Many Americans were shocked both at My Lai and at the subsequent penalty meted to platoon leader Calley. While Americans could fathom atrocities committed by other nations it was a rude awakening to learn that fellow countrymen would commit such horrendous acts.

Man and Message
Isaiah 40:3
Mark 1:2-6, Luke 3:3-14
2 And saying, Repent; for the kingdom of heaven is at hand.
3 For this is he that was spoken of by the prophet, Isaiah, saying, The voice of one crying in the wilderness, Prepare ye the way of the Lord, make His paths straight.
4 And the same John had his raiment of camel's hair, and a leather belt about his waist; and his food was locusts and wild honey.
5 Then went out to him Jerusalem, and all Judaea, and all the region round about *the* Jordan,
6 And were baptized by him in *the* Jordan, confessing their sins.
7 But when he saw many of the Pharisees and Sadducees come to his baptism, he said unto them, O generation of vipers, who hath warned you to flee from the wrath to come?
8 Bring forth, therefore, fruits befitting repentance.
9 And think not to say within yourselves, We have Abraham as *our* father; for I say unto you that God is able of these stones to raise up children unto Abraham.
10 And now also the axe is laid unto the root of the trees; therefore, every tree which bringeth not forth good fruit is hewn down, and cast into the fire.

His Courage
Luke 3:19-20
11 I, indeed, baptize you with water unto repentance, but He who cometh after me is mightier than I, whose shoes I am not worthy to bear; He shall baptize you with the Holy Spirit, and *with* fire;
¹ 12 Whose fan *is* in His hand, and He will thoroughly purge His floor, and gather His wheat into the granary, but He will burn up the chaff with unquenchable fire.

¹ (3:12) Revelation 20:11-15.

Jesus Baptized
c. 27 A.D.
● *Jordan*
Mark 1:9-11, Luke 3:21-23,
John 1:29-34, Psalm 2:7
13 Then cometh Jesus from Galilee to *the* Jordan unto John, to be baptized by him.
14 But John forbade Him, saying, I have need to be baptized of thee, and comest thou to me?
15 And Jesus answering said unto him, Permit *it to be so* now; for thus it becometh us to fulfill all righteousness. Then he consented *to* Him.
16 And Jesus, when He was baptized, went up straightway out of the water; and, lo, the heavens were opened unto Him, and He saw the Spirit of God descending like a dove, and lighting upon Him.
17 And, lo, a voice from heaven, saying, This is my beloved Son, in whom I am well pleased.

CHAPTER 4

Jesus Tempted
● *Wilderness of Judea*
Mark 1:12-13, Luke 4:1-13,
Psalm 91:11
1 Then was Jesus led up by the Spirit into the wilderness to be tested by the devil.
2 And when He had fasted forty days and forty nights, He was afterward hungry.
3 And when the tempter came to Him, He said, If thou be the Son of God, command that these stones be made bread.
4 But He answered and said, It is written, Man shall not live by bread alone, but by every word that proceedeth out of the mouth of God.
5 Then the devil taketh Him up into the holy city, and setteth Him on a pinnacle of the temple,
6 And saith unto Him, If thou be the Son of God, cast thyself down; for it

(Matthew 3:7)

THE PHARISEES and SADDUCEES

The Pharisees were a sect. They originated during the Intertestament Period, in the 2nd Century B.C. [The period between The Old and New Testament]. They came from out of the "Pious Ones" who fought with the Maccabees against Antiochus IV, the Syrian tyrant who desecrated the Temple in 169 B.C. Their name means "separated-ones" and by the time of Chirst they had fallen into the sins of self-righteousness and hypocrisy. They were the most numerous and influential of the religious sects of Jesus' day. They were self-denying and stood for the strict observance of the Old Testament law.

The Sadducees were also a Jewish sect. They too originated in the Intertestament Period, but their precise source is much debated. The name in the Hebrew means, "righteous-ones." They, however, denied the existence of angels, and did not believe in the resurrection of the body. They denied all miracles. They believed only in the written law whereas the Pharisees also upheld the oral traditions.

Mrs. Diana Pike, widow of former Episcopal Bishop James A. Pike, places her hands on his coffin at St. Peter's Cemetery in Jaffa, Israel.

(Matthew 4:1)

THE TERRORS OF THE WILDERNESS

Spending just one night in the Judean wilderness can be a frightening experience. Jesus spent 40 days there! Nights can be windy and cold. Days become unbearably hot reaching as high as 125°.

The controversial theologian, Bishop James A. Pike died September 7, 1970 when he and his wife became lost in the desert hills of Judea. Perhaps by no other recent event has the treachery of the Holy Land desert been brought so vividly to our attention.

It is interesting to note that Christ defeated Satan in this temptation period through using the Word of God (Matthew 4:4,7). What a lesson for us when we are tempted!

Author is pictured here in front of ruins at Capernaum.

(Matthew 4:13)

CAPERNAUM...WHERE JESUS BEGINS HIS PUBLIC MINISTRY

Capernaum is about 90 miles from Jerusalem and is located on the northwest shore of the Sea of Galilee. This is where Jesus made His headquarters during His ministry in Galilee.

Jesus performed many miracles here and it was here that He called Matthew to the apostleship. This is also where the discourse on the Bread of Life was delivered, after Jesus fed the 5000 (John 6:24).

The remains of a synagogue, probably from the first century and then rebuilt, are about all that is left in this historic area.

is written, He shall give His angels charge concerning thee, and in *their* hands they shall bear thee up, lest at any time thou dash thy foot against a stone.

7 Jesus said unto him, It is written again, Thou shalt not put the Lord, thy God, to the test.

8 Again, the devil taketh Him up into an exceedingly high mountain, and showeth Him all the kingdoms of the world, and the glory of them,

9 And saith unto Him, All these things will I give thee, if thou wilt fall down and worship me.

10 Then saith Jesus unto him, Begone, Satan; for it is written, Thou shalt worship the Lord, thy God, and Him only shalt thou serve.

11 Then the devil leaveth Him, and, behold, angels came and ministered unto Him.

Leaves for Galilee
Early 28 A.D.
● *Judea*
Mark 1:14, Luke 4:14,
John 3:22-30, 4:1-4

12 Now when Jesus had heard that John was cast into prison, He departed into Galilee;

13 And leaving Nazareth, He came and dwelt in Capernaum, which is upon the seacoast, in the borders of Zebulun and Naphtali,

Moved to Capernaum
● *Capernaum*
Isaiah 9:1-2

14 That it might be fulfilled which was spoken by Isaiah, the prophet, saying,

15 The land of Zebulun, and the land of Naphtali, *by* the way of the sea, beyond *the* Jordan, Galilee of the nations;

16 The people who sat in darkness saw great light, and to them who sat in the region and shadow of death, light is sprung up.

17 From that time Jesus began to preach, and to say, Repent; for the kingdom of heaven is at hand.

4 Become Fishers of Men
● *Sea of Galilee*
Mark 1:16-20, Luke 5:1-11,
Psalm 33:9

18 And Jesus, walking by the Sea of Galilee, saw two brethren, Simon, called Peter, and Andrew, his brother, casting a net into the sea; for they were fishers.

19 And He saith unto them, Follow me, and I will make you fishers of men.

20 And they straightway left *their* nets, and followed Him.

21 And going on from there, He saw two other brethren, James, *the son* of Zebedee, and John, his brother, in a boat with Zebedee, their father, mending their nets; and He called them.

22 And they immediately left the boat and their father, and followed Him.

First Preaching Tour of Galilee
28 A.D.
● *Galilee*
Mark 1:35-39,
Luke 4:42-44

23 And Jesus went about all Galilee, teaching in their synagogues, and preaching the gospel of the kingdom, and healing all manner of sickness and all manner of disease among the people.

24 And His fame went throughout all Syria; and they brought unto Him all sick people that were taken with diverse diseases and torments, and those who were possessed with demons, and those who were epileptics, and those who had the palsy; and He healed them.

25 And there followed Him great multitudes of people from Galilee, and *from* Decapolis, and *from* Jerusalem, and *from* Judaea, and *from* beyond *the* Jordan.

PAST	PRESENT	RAPTURE	FIRST 3½ LAST 3½ TRIBULATION	ARMA-GEDDON	MIL-LENNIUM	NEW HEAVENS & EARTH

(Matthew 4:9)

The week of February 21st, 1972, President Nixon went to Red China. Upon his return he declared that "This was the week we changed the world."

His trip was hailed by his administration as a "Journey for Peace." In 1938 Neville Chamberlain, with umbrella, went to Munich to negotiate with Adolf Hitler. This effort to win peace failed.

It is a sad commentary on today's world when anti-God countries such as Red China and Russia can woo American leaders into believing an alliance with evil can produce good. The President's "Journey for Peace" could well be the initial step that starts the United States downhill as a follower...no longer a leader. If this be true look for the United States to eventually join the Common Market countries in a United States of Europe.

CHAPTER 5

**Sermon on the Mount
(Chapters 5-7)**
● *Near Capernaum*
Luke 6:20-49

1 And seeing the multitudes, He went up into a mountain: and when He was seated, His disciples came unto Him.
2 And He opened His mouth, and taught them, saying,
3 Blessed *are* the poor in spirit; for theirs is the kingdom of heaven.
4 Blessed *are* they that mourn; for they shall be comforted.
5 Blessed *are* the meek; for they shall inherit the earth.
6 Blessed *are* they who do hunger and thirst after righteousness; for they shall be filled.
7 Blessed *are* the merciful; for they shall obtain mercy.
8 Blessed *are* the pure in heart; for they shall see God.
9 Blessed *are* the peacemakers; for they shall be called the sons of God.
10 Blessed *are* they who are persecuted for righteousness' sake; for theirs is the kingdom of heaven.
11 Blessed are ye, when *men* shall revile you, and persecute *you*, and shall say all manner of evil against you falsely, for My sake.
12 Rejoice, and be exceedingly glad; for great *is* your reward in heaven; for so persecuted they the prophets who were before you.
13 Ye are the salt of the earth, but if the salt have lost its savor, with what shall it be salted? It is thereafter good for nothing, but to be cast out, and to be trodden under foot of men.
14 Ye are the light of the world. A city that is set on an hill cannot be hidden.

15 Neither do men light a lamp, and put it under a bushel, but on a lampstand, and it giveth light unto all that are in the house.
16 Let your light so shine before men, that they may see your good works, and glorify your Father, who is in heaven.
17 Think not that I am come to destroy the law, or the prophets; I am not come to destroy, but to fulfill.
18 For verily I say unto you, Till heaven and earth pass, one jot or one tittle shall in no way pass from the law, till all be fulfilled. 1
19 Whosoever, therefore, shall break one of these least commandments, and shall teach men so, he shall be called the least in the kingdom of heaven; but whosoever shall do and teach *them,* the same shall be called great in the kingdom of heaven.
20 For I say unto you that except your righteousness shall exceed *the righteousness* of the scribes and Pharisees, ye shall in no case enter into the kingdom of heaven.
21 Ye have heard that it was said by them of old, Thou shalt not kill and whosoever shall kill shall be in danger of judgment;
22 But I say unto you that 2 whosoever is angry with his brother without a cause shall be in danger of judgment; and whosoever shall say to his brother, Raca, shall be in danger of the council; but whosoever shall say, Thou fool, shall be in danger of hell fire.
23 Therefore, if thou bring thy gift to the altar, and there rememberest that thy brother hath anything against thee,
24 Leave there thy gift before the altar, and go thy way; first be reconciled to thy brother, and then come and offer thy gift.

1   (5:18) II Peter 3:10 and Revelation 21:1. This endurance of Scripture has been fulfilled in the past, and it shall be fulfilled in the present and future.

2   (5:22) Revelation 20:11-15.

PAST	PRESENT	RAPTURE	FIRST 3½ LAST 3½ TRIBULATION	ARMA-GEDDON	MIL-LENNIUM	NEW HEAVENS & EARTH

Sea of Galilee and Plain of Gennesaret from Hattin, Mt. of Beatitudes. It was in this area that the Crusaders were routed by Saladin, October 2, 1187 A.D.

(Matthew 5:1)

The Horns of Hattin, a rocky hill near the Sea of Galilee. This site is located 7 miles west of Tiberias. Here at this spot in 1187 A.D. the forces of Islam under the leadership of Saladin slaughtered the Crusaders who were led by Guy de Lusignan. This decisive defeat was the turning point within the crusades which saw the forces of the West finally routed from the Holy Land.

Philippine men allow themselves to be tortured believing that such steps will atone them for their sins and assure them a place in Heaven.

(Matthew 5:13)

SALT CAN PENETRATE THE SIN OF THE WORLD

Edmund Burke declared, "The only thing necessary for the triumph of evil is for good men to do nothing about it."

The Saviour dealt sternly with the sin of do-nothingism (Matthew 25:25-30). What could a handful of apostles do to evangelize a world? In themselves, nothing! But with God...they become as salt...a few crystals sprinkled here and there over the "meat" of the world...can reach down and penetrate the world, purifying the heart (Acts 2:37). The gospel becomes the salt of grace. And Christians, who become shining lights for God, are the salt of the earth.

THE UNSAVED DEAD BEFORE
THEIR JUDGMENT DAY

What happens to those unbelievers who have already died, who will die today, tomorrow or anytime in the future before their Final Judgment after the 1000 year Millennium?

Dr. J. Dwight Pentecost in his book THINGS TO COME points out that there are four different words used in Scriptures to describe the place of the dead until their resurrection at the Great White Throne Judgment at the close of the Millennium.

These four words do NOT always refer to the eternal state of "the Lake of Fire" (which begins after the 1000 year Millennium) but rather often to the temporary place in which the dead await their resurrection. Here are those words:

1. SHEOL
    This is used 65 times in the Old Testament of which 31 times it is translated "grave."

2. HADES (literally, the "unseen" world.)
    This is used generally to describe the unsaved dead who are awaiting the resurrection unto the Great White Throne. In every instance but one it is translated as "hell."

3. TARTAROS
    This word is only used once in Scripture (2 Peter 2:4) and refers to the judgment on the wicked angels.

4. GEHENNA
    This is used 12 times in the New Testament.
    (Matthew 5:22, 29-30, Mark 9:43, etc)
    [In the Hebrew this word literally means "Valley" *(Ge)* "of Hennon" *(Henna)*. Its fires burning the garbage of Jerusalem provided Christ with the perfect picture of the eternal doom of those who are lost.]

The unbelieving dead are right now in torment and in misery in their temporary place of punishment — Hades or Hell (Luke 16:19-31). Here they await their final resurrection after the 1000 year Millennial reign of Christ which will then be immediately followed by the Great White Throne judgment and their eternal condemnation to the Lake of Fire (Revelation 20:11-15).

25 Agree with thine adversary quickly, while thou art in the way with him, lest at any time the adversary deliver thee to the judge, and the judge deliver thee to the officer, and thou be cast into prison.

26 Verily I say unto thee, Thou shalt by no means come out from there, till thou hast paid the uttermost farthing.

27 Ye have heard that it was said by them of old, Thou shalt not commit adultery;

28 But I say unto you that whosoever looketh on a woman to lust after her hath committed adultery with her already in his heart.

29 And if thy right eye offend thee, pluck it out, and cast *it* from thee; for it is profitable for thee that one of thy members should perish, and not *that* thy whole body should be cast into hell.

30 And if thy right hand offend thee, cut it off, and cast *it* from thee; for it is profitable for thee that one of thy members should perish, and not *that* thy whole body should be cast into hell.

31 It hath been said, Whosoever shall put away his wife, let him give her a writing of divorcement;

32 But I say unto you that whosoever shall put away his wife, except for the cause of fornication, causeth her to commit adultery; and whosoever shall marry her that is divorced committeth adultery.

33 Again, ye have heard that it hath been said by them of old, Thou shalt not perjure thyself, but shalt perform unto the Lord thine oaths;

34 But I say unto you, Swear not at all; neither by heaven, for it is God's throne;

35 Nor by the earth, for it is His footstool; neither by Jerusalem, for it is the city of the great King.

36 Neither shalt thou swear by thy head, because thou canst not make one hair white or black.

37 But let your communication be, Yea, yea; Nay, nay; for whatever is more than these cometh of evil.

38 Ye have heard that it hath been said, An eye for an eye, and a tooth for a tooth;

39 But I say unto you that ye resist not evil, but whosoever shall smite thee on thy right cheek, turn to him the other also.

40 And if any man will sue thee at the law, and take away thy coat, let him have *thy* cloak also.

41 And whosoever shall compel thee to go a mile, go with him two.

42 Give to him that asketh thee, and from him that would borrow of thee turn not thou away.

43 Ye have heard that it hath been said, Thou shalt love thy neighbor, and hate thine enemy;

44 But I say unto you, Love your enemies, bless them that curse you, do good to them that hate you, and pray for them who despitefully use you, and persecute you,

45 That ye may be the sons of your Father, who is in heaven; for He maketh His sun to rise on the evil and on the good, and sendeth rain on the just and on the unjust.

46 For if ye love them who love you, what reward have ye? Do not even the tax collectors the same?

47 And if ye greet your brethren only, what do ye more *than others?* Do not even the heathen so?

48 Be ye, therefore, perfect, even as your Father, who is in heaven, is perfect.

CHAPTER 6

1 Take heed that ye do not your alms before men, to be seen by them; otherwise ye have no reward of your Father, who is in heaven.

2 Therefore, when thou doest *thine* alms, do not sound a trumpet before thee, as the hypocrites do in the synagogues and in the streets, that they may have glory from men. Verily I say unto you, They have their reward.

PAST	PRESENT	RAPTURE	FIRST 3½ LAST 3½ TRIBULATION		ARMA-GEDDON	MIL-LENNIUM	NEW HEAVENS & EARTH

Premarital Conceptions Found High

By NAN ROBERTSON
Special to The New York Times

WASHINGTON, April 7 — One-third of all first-born children in the United States from 1964 through 1966 were conceived out of wedlock, a Government survey disclosed today.

Hastily arranged marriages gave many babies legitimacy by the time of their birth, but one out of every seven was born illegitimate during that period.

These were among the major findings of an extraordinary report from the Department of Health, Education and Welfare, based on a solid sampling of one out of every 1,000 first births in those years. It was the first attempt in this country to obtain national estimates of extramarital conception.

These were among the major conclusions of an extraordinary report from the Department of Health, Education and Welfare, based on a solid sampling of one out of every 1,000 first births in those years. It was the first attempt in this country to obtain national estimates of exramarital conception, according to Mrs. Mary Grace Kovar, a leading analyst for the Division of Vital Statistics.

The study, conducted by the National Center for Health Statistics, pointed up a connection between income and pregnancy at the time of marriage.

More than 37 per cent of women in families earning less than $3,000 a year went to the altar pregnant. A shade more than 8 per cent from families with income exceeding $10,000 were expecting when married.

Forty-two per cent of the married women under 20 had been wed less than eight months when their first baby was born.

The size of the sample was 11,331 first births out of 1.1 million in the United States annually from 1964 through 1966.

Statistics are being gathered for more recent years, but the data have not been tabulated.

Those who took the last survey said there was no way to predict now whether newer figures would show more, less or the same number of illegitimate babies. They cited as imponderables the effects of the birth control pill and increasing sexual freedom.

The central finding of the 1964-66 National Natality Survey is the following:

"If the assumption is made as being within eight months of first marriages were indeed pre-marital conceptions, then the data from the . . . survey indicate that of the average 1,174,000 first births to women aged 15-44 which occurred in the United States each year during 1964-66, 166,000, or 14 per cent, were illegitimate and

---

(Matthew 5:27)

PREMARITAL CONCEPTIONS FOUND HIGH

A Government survey has disclosed that one-third of all first-born children in the United States are conceived out of wedlock.

And 42% of the married women under 20 had been wed less than eight months when their first baby was born. It is estimated that almost 18% of the first births to women in the U.S. were illegitimate and 15% were pre-marital conceptions of legitimate babies. Thus an annual average of some 400,000 first births are conceived outside marriage!

(Matthew 5:44)

LOVE YOUR ENEMIES

Sometimes a photograph conveys more than anything else the hate that can build up in a world which is not committed to Christ. Photo shows former South Vietnamese police chief Gen. Nguyen Ngoc Loan executing a Viet Cong officer with a single pistol shot in the head. The Viet Cong officer grimaces at the impact of the fatal bullet.

Typical Arab market still uses balancing scales. Is our life and testimony weighed in the balances and found wanting?

(Matthew 5:48)

THE FATHER IN HEAVEN IS PERFECT

That man can achieve absolute perfection is not implied here. God alone is absolutely perfect and is the standard of perfection. Yet God's command puts forth this as the goal. The word "perfect" used here implies full development and growth into maturity. Read Ephesians 4:13, Colossians 1:28; 4:12. Even Paul denied that he had attained absolute perfection (Philippians 3:12). Hebrews 2:10 tells us that the sinless Christ was perfected through suffering.

3 But when thou doest alms, let not thy left hand know what thy right hand doeth,

4 That thine alms may be in secret; and thy Father, who seeth in secret, shall reward thee openly.

5 And when thou prayest, thou shalt not be as the hypocrites *are;* for they love to pray standing in the synagogues and at the corners of the streets, that they may be seen by men. Verily I say unto you, They have their reward.

6 But thou, when thou prayest, enter into thy room, and when thou hast shut thy door, pray to thy Father, who is in secret; and thy Father, who seeth in secret, shall reward thee openly.

7 But when ye pray, use not vain repetitions, as the pagans *do;* for they think that they shall be heard for their much speaking.

8 Be not ye, therefore, like unto them; for your Father knoweth what things ye have need of, before ye ask Him.

9 After this manner, therefore, pray ye: Our Father, who art in heaven, Hallowed be thy name.

1 10 Thy kingdom come. Thy will be done in earth, as *it is* in heaven.

11 Give us this day our daily bread.

12 And forgive us our debts, as we forgive our debtors.

13 And lead us not into temptation, but deliver us from evil. For thine is the kingdom, and the power, and the glory, forever. Amen.

2 14 For if ye forgive men their trespasses, your heavenly Father will also forgive you;

15 But if ye forgive not men their trespasses, neither will your Father forgive your trespasses.

16 Moreover, when ye fast, be not, as the hypocrites, of a sad countenance; for they disfigure their faces, that they may appear unto men to fast. Verily I say unto you, They have their reward.

17 But thou, when thou fastest, anoint thine head, and wash thy face,

18 That thou appear not unto men to fast, but unto thy Father, who is in secret; and thy Father, who seeth in secret, shall reward thee openly.

Lay Up Treasures in Heaven

19 Lay not up for yourselves treasures upon earth, where moth and rust doth corrupt, and where thieves break through and steal,

20 But lay up for yourselves treasures in heaven, where neither moth nor rust doth corrupt, and where thieves do not break through nor steal;

21 For where your treasure is, there will your heart be also.

22 The lamp of the body is the eye; if, therefore, thine eye be healthy, thy whole body shall be full of light.

23 But if thine eye be evil, thy whole body shall be full of darkness. If, therefore, the light that *is* in thee be darkness, how great *is* that darkness!

24 No man can serve two masters; for either he will hate the one, and love the other; or else he will hold to the one, and despise the other. Ye cannot serve God and money.

Avoid Anxiety

25 Therefore, I say unto you, Be not anxious for your life, what ye shall eat, or what ye shall drink; nor yet for your body, what ye shall put on. Is not the life more than food and the body than raiment?

26 Behold the fowls of the air; for they sow not, neither do they reap, nor gather into barns, yet your heavenly Father feedeth them. Are ye not much better than they?

27 Which of you by being anxious can add one cubit unto his stature?

1 (6:10) God's Kingdom is both present and future.

2 (6:14-15) For we must all appear before the judgment seat of Christ; that every one may receive the things done in his body, according to that he hath done, whether it be good or bad (II Corinthians 5:10). This is addressed by Christ primarily to His followers.

28 And why are ye anxious for raiment? Consider the lilies of the field, how they grow; they toil not, neither do they spin,
29 And yet I say unto you that even Solomon, in all his glory, was not arrayed like one of these.
30 Wherefore, if God so clothe the grass of the field, which today is, and tomorrow is cast into the oven, *shall He* not much more *clothe* you, O ye of little faith?
31 Therefore, be not anxious saying, What shall we eat? or, What shall we drink? or, With what shall we be clothed?
32 For after all these things do the Gentiles seek. For your heavenly Father knoweth that ye have need of all these things.
1 33 But seek ye first the kingdom of God, and His righteousness, and all these things shall be added unto you.
34 Be, therefore, not anxious about tomorrow; for tomorrow will be anxious for the things of itself. Sufficient unto the day *is* its own evil.

CHAPTER 7

1 Judge not, that ye be not judged.
2 For with what judgment ye judge, ye shall be judged; and with what measure ye measure, it shall be measured to you again.
3 And why beholdest thou the mote that is in thy brother's eye, but considerest not the beam that is in thine own eye?
4 Or how wilt thou say to thy brother, Let me pull the mote out of thine eye; and, behold, a beam *is* in thine own eye?
5 Thou hypocrite, first cast the beam out of thine own eye, and then shalt thou see clearly to cast the mote out of thy brother's eye.

6 Give not that which is holy unto the dogs, neither cast your pearls before swine, lest they trample them under their feet, and turn again and lacerate you.
7 Ask, and it shall be given you; seek, and ye shall find; knock, and it shall be opened unto you;
8 For every one that asketh receiveth; and he that seeketh findeth; and to him that knocketh it shall be opened.
9 Or what man is there of you whom, if his son ask bread, will he give him a stone?
10 Or if he ask a fish, will he give him a serpent?
11 If ye then, being evil, know how to give good gifts unto your children, how much more shall your Father, who is in heaven, give good things to them that ask Him?
12 Therefore, all things whatever ye would that men should do to you, do ye even so to them; for this is the law and the prophets.
13 Enter in at the narrow gate; for wide *is* the gate, and broad *is* the way, that leadeth to destruction, and many there be who go in *that way;*
14 Because narrow *is* the gate, and hard *is* the way, which leadeth unto life, and few there be that find it.
15 Beware of false prophets, who come to you in sheep's clothing, but inwardly they are ravening wolves.
16 Ye shall know them by their fruits. Do men gather grapes of thorns, or figs of thistles?
17 Even so, every good tree bringeth forth good fruit, but a corrupt tree bringeth forth bad fruit.
18 A good tree cannot bring forth bad fruit, neither *can* a corrupt tree bring forth good fruit.
19 Every tree that bringeth not forth good fruit is hewn down, and cast into the fire.

---

1   (6:33) Today and in the world to come.

PAST	PRESENT	RAPTURE	FIRST 3½ LAST 3½ TRIBULATION	ARMA-GEDDON	MIL-LENNIUM	NEW HEAVENS & EARTH

(Matthew 6:16)

THE HYPOCRISY OF SANCTIMONY

Those who fast and make their faces unsightly, appearing gloomy-faced for the entire world to see, are like hypocrites who make a show of their piety. It is one thing to sanctify one's life...but an entirely different thing to be sanctimonious. **Sanctify** implies a consecration to God. Sanctimony is making a hypocritical show...like the Pharisees. Isaiah 65:5 warns, "(Those) which say, Stand by thyself, come not near to me; for I am holier than thou. These are a smoke in my nose, a fire that burneth all the day."

Americans pay out almost $30 million annually on water skiing.

(Matthew 6:20)

$90 BILLION FOR LEISURE

Affluent Americans with more time on their hands and money to spend than ever before, have boomed leisure into an over 90-billion-dollar business this year.

Pleasure industries have been growing at an average rate of nearly $6 billion a year since 1965. As an example Americans pay out almost 30 million annually on water skiing. They bought almost 10 million dollars' worth of surfboards last year.

Hand in hand down a country lane a child holds her father's hand. Are you fully placing your life in the hand of the Lord?

(Matthew 7:7)

GOD'S BLANK CHECK

There are over 7000 promises in the Bible. The problem with many Christians is that they are so overwhelmed they sometimes forget to "cash God's check." How important it is to claim God's promises for your life **ONE BY ONE.** And Matthew 7:7,8 would be a good place for you to start. Simply claim one promise a week and you will be kept busy for a lifetime! And remember Psalm 37:5 which reminds us to "Commit thy way unto the Lord; trust also in Him, and He shall bring it to pass."

20 Wherefore, by their fruits ye shall know them.

1 21 Not every one that saith unto Me, Lord, Lord, shall enter into the kingdom of heaven, but he that doeth the will of My Father, who is in heaven.

22 Many will say to Me in that day, Lord, Lord, have we not prophesied in thy name? And in thy name have cast our demons? And in thy name done many wonderful works?

23 And then will I profess unto them, I never knew you; depart from Me, ye that work iniquity.

24 Therefore, whosoever heareth these sayings of Mine, and doeth them, I will liken him unto a wise man, who built his house upon a rock.

25 And the rain descended, and the floods came, and the winds blew and beat upon that house, and it fell not; for it was founded upon a rock.

26 And every one that heareth these sayings of Mine, and doeth them not, shall be likened unto a foolish man, who built his house upon the sand.

27 And the rain descended, and the floods came, and the winds blew and beat upon that house, and it fell; and great was the fall of it.

28 And it came to pass, when Jesus had ended these sayings, the people were astonished at His doctrine.

29 For He taught them as one having authority, and not as the scribes.

CHAPTER 8

1 When He was come down from the mountain, great multitudes followed Him.

**Leper Healed
and Response Recorded**
● *Galilee*
Mark 1:40-45
Luke 5:12-16
Lev. 13:49

2 And, behold, there came a leper and worshiped Him, saying, Lord, if thou wilt, thou canst make me clean.

3 And Jesus put forth *His* hand, and touched him, saying, I will; be thou clean. And immediately his leprosy was cleansed.

4 And Jesus saith unto him, See thou tell no man, but go thy way, show thyself to the priest, and offer the gift that Moses commanded, for a testimony unto them.

Centurion's Servant Healed
● *Capernaum*
Luke 7:1-10
Isaiah 49:12

5 And when Jesus was entered into Capernaum, there came unto Him a centurion, beseeching Him.

6 And saying, Lord, my servant lieth at home sick of the palsy, grievously tormented.

7 And Jesus saith unto him, I will come and heal him.

8 The centurion answered and said, Lord, I am not worthy that thou shouldest come under my·roof; but speak the word only, and my servant shall be healed.

9 For I am a man under authority, having soldiers under me; and I say to this *man,* Go, and he goeth; and to another, Come, and he cometh; and to my servant, Do this, and he doeth *it.*

10 When Jesus heard *it,* He marveled, and said to them that followed, Verily I say unto you, I have not found so great faith, no, not in Israel.

11 And I say unto you that many shall come from the east and west, and shall sit down with Abraham, and Isaac, and Jacob, in the kingdom of heaven;

12 But the sons of the kingdom shall be cast out into outer darkness; there shall be weeping and gnashing of teeth.

13 And Jesus said unto the centurion, Go thy way; and as thou hast believed, *so* be it done unto thee. And his servant was healed in the very same hour.

1　(7:21-23) Great White Throne Judgment. Revelation 20:11-15.

Peter's Mother-in-Law
Cured Plus Others
c. Autumn 28 A.D.
- *Capernaum*
Mark 1:29-34
Luke 4:38-41
Isaiah 53:4

14 And when Jesus was come into Peter's house, He saw his wife's mother lying, and sick of a fever.

15 And He touched her hand, and the fever left her; and she arose, and ministered unto Him.

16 When the evening was come, they brought unto Him many that were possessed with demons; and He cast out the spirits with *His* word, and healed all that were sick,

1   17 That it might be fulfilled what was spoken by Isaiah, the prophet, saying, He Himself took our infirmities, and bore *our* sicknesses.

The Test of Discipleship
- *Capernaum*
Matthew 18:1-35
Mark 9:33-50
Luke 9:46-62

18 Now, when Jesus saw great multitudes about Him, He gave commandment to depart unto the other side.

19 And a certain scribe came, and said unto Him, Master, I will follow thee wherever thou goest.

20 And Jesus saith unto him, The foxes have holes, and the birds of the air *have* nests, but the Son of man hath not where to lay *His* head.

21 And another of His disciples said unto Him, Lord, permit me first to go and bury my father.

22 But Jesus said unto him, Follow Me, and let the dead bury their dead.

Sea Made Serene
- *Sea of Galilee*
Mark 4:35-41
Luke 8:22-25

23 And when He was entered into a boat, His disciples followed Him.

24 And, behold, there arose a great tempest in the sea, insomuch that the boat was covered with the waves; but He was asleep.

25 And His disciples came to *Him,* and awoke Him, saying, Lord, save us; we perish.

26 And He saith unto them, Why are ye fearful, O ye of little faith? Then He arose, and rebuked the winds and the sea; and there was a great calm.

27 But the men marveled, saying, What manner of man is this, that even the winds and the sea obey Him?

Gadarene Demoniac Healed
- *E. Shore of Galilee*
Mark 5:1-20
Luke 8:26-39

28 And when He was come to the other side into the country of the Gadarenes, there met Him two possessed with demons, coming out of the tombs, exceedingly fierce, so that no man might pass by that way.

29 And, behold, they cried out, saying, What have we to do with thee, Jesus, thou Son of God? Art thou come here to torment us before the time?

30 And there was a good way off from them an herd of many swine feeding.

31 So the demons besought Him, saying, If thou cast us out, permit us to go away into the herd of swine.

---

1   (8:17) Surely He hath borne our griefs, and carried our sorrows: yet we did esteem Him stricken, smitten of God, and afflicted (Isaiah 53:4). Jesus' healing those who were physically ill fulfills this Old Testament prophecy that the Messiah would take away the infirmities of those who would trust in Him. This Old Testament passage, however, in context speaks also of and primarily of, Christ's bearing our sins at His death.

PAST	PRESENT	RAPTURE	FIRST 3½ LAST 3½ TRIBULATION		ARMA-GEDDON	MIL-LENNIUM	NEW HEAVENS & EARTH

A Christian should be discerning, able to distinguish the wheat from the chaff. In the Last Days false teachings will flourish.

(Matthew 7:15)

DECEPTIVE CULTS FLOURISHING

It is important that Christians remain stedfast in the Word of God and not be led astray by every wind of doctrine that passes their way. If Christians **know** the Word of God they will learn to discern the difference between the teaching of false prophets and Scripture.

One cult, known as Anglo-Israelism, whose chief proponent publishes THE PLAIN TRUTH magazine, has an operating budget of over $50 MILLION a year and is growing at a fantastic rate. They receive as much as a QUARTER MILLION letters a month...and are heard over 300 radio stations and 50 television stations. THE PLAIN TRUTH has a circulation well over 2 million copies.

(Matthew 7:22)

DEMONS...and HOW SATAN'S AGENTS WORK

Demons operate above the laws of the natural realm. They are invisible and without material substance.

1. Demons are spirits. See Matthew 12:43,45.

2. Demons are numerous...so numerous that Mark 5:9 describes one demon as saying. "My name is Legion: for we are many."

   A Legion was the largest single unit in the Roman army, including infantry and cavalry. A legion of infantry at full strength consisted of about 6000 Roman soldiers. In the New Testament the term "legion" represents a vast number.

3. Demons can control men. See Mark 5:2-5.

4. Demons are unclean and violent (Matthew 8:28-31).

5. Demons know Jesus Christ as the Most High God. They recognize His supreme authority. See Mark 1:23,24; Acts 19:15, James 2:19.

6. They are aware of their eternal fate. "And, behold, they cried out, saying, What have we to do with thee, Jesus, thou Son of God? Art thou come here to torment us before the time?" (Matthew 8:29).

7. Demons are in conflict with spiritual Christians. See Ephesians 6:12. Also "Now the Spirit speaketh expressly that, in the latter times, some shall depart from the faith, giving heed to seducing spirits, and doctrines of demons..." (1 Timothy 4:1).

8. Unbelievers are susceptible to demon possession.
   "And you (believers) hath He made alive who were dead in trespasses and sins; In which in times past ye walked according to the course of this world, according to the prince of the power of the air, the spirit that now worketh in the sons of disobedience" (Ephesians 2:1,2).

9. After Christ comes again for His Church at the Rapture of the Saints, this present Age will end in the Tribulation Period with an emergence of demons. Read Revelation 9:1-11,20.

Demons are some type of fallen angelic beings possessing terrible strength, imparting it to the human body in such forms as blindness (Matthew 12:22), insanity (Luke 8:26-36), dumbness (Matthew 9:32,33) and suicidal mania (Mark 9:22). However, it must be kept in mind that not every physical nor mental affliction is a result of demonism. Demonism is under the leadership of Satan and as such seeks to oppose God's purposes and to hinder man's welfare.

That Christ actually spoke to the demons and heard their replies shows that they are real beings and not merely ancient ways to describe illnesses (Matthew 8:28-34). It is probable that demonic activity reached its height while Christ was on earth—as it will again during the Tribulation.

"Now when the Centurion saw what was done, he glorified God, saying Certainly this was a righteous man" (Luke 23:47).

(Matthew 8:5)

CENTURION FOLLOWS CHRIST

A Centurion was a commander of 100 men in the Roman Army. Five are mentioned in the New Testament. Three of them became followers of Christ. They were (1) the unnamed Centurion of verses 5-8. He was characterized by humility, in spite of his position of leadership; by his faith in Christ; and by his devotion to his sick servant. (2) The Roman Centurion assigned to duty close to the cross of Christ during His Crucifixion (Mark 15:39). (3) The Centurion named Cornelius stationed with the Italian band at Caesarea (Acts 10:2).

Peaceful cruise across the Sea of Galilee.

(Matthew 8:24)

DANGEROUS SQUALLS IN GALILEE

The Sea of Galilee is located some 60 miles north of Jerusalem. It varies in depth up to 150 feet. Its greatest width is 8 miles at Magdala and it runs a little over 13 miles in length.

The Sea of Galilee is noted for its sudden and violent storms. This is caused by cold air sweeping down the plateaus of Mt. Hermon and other mountains, through the ravines and gorges, converging at the head of the lake where it meets warm air.

32 And He said unto them, Go. And when they were come out, they went into the herd of swine; and, behold, the whole herd of swine ran violently down a steep place into the sea, and perished in the waters.

33 And they that kept them fled, and went their ways into the city, and told everything, and what was befallen to *those* possessed with the demons.

34 And, behold, the whole city came out to meet Jesus; and when they saw Him, they besought *Him* that He would depart from their borders.

CHAPTER 9

Paralytic Healed
● *Capernaum*
Mark 2:1-12
Luke 5:17-20
Romans 3:23

1 And He entered into a boat, and passed over, and came into His own city.

2 And, behold, they brought to Him a man sick of the palsy, lying on a bed; and Jesus, seeing their faith, said unto the sick of the palsy, Son, be of good cheer; thy sins be forgiven thee.

3 And, behold, certain of the scribes said within themselves, This *man* blasphemeth.

4 And Jesus, knowing their thoughts, said, Why think ye evil in your hearts?

5 For which is easier, to say, *Thy* sins be forgiven thee; or to say, Arise, and walk?

6 But that ye may know that the Son of man hath power on earth to forgive sins (then saith He to the sick of the palsy), Arise, take up thy bed, and go unto thine house.

7 And he arose, and departed to his house.

8 But when the multitudes saw *it,* they marveled, and glorified God, who had given such power unto men.

Matthew's Call and Reception Dinner
● *Capernaum*
Mark 2:13-17
Luke 5:27-32
Hosea 6:6

9 And as Jesus passed forth from there, He saw a man, named Matthew, sitting at the tax office; and He saith unto him, Follow Me, And he arose, and followed Him.

10 And it came to pass, as Jesus sat eating in the house, behold, many tax collectors and sinners came and sat down with Him and His disciples.

11 And when the Pharisees saw *it,* they said unto His disciples, Why eateth your Master with tax collectors and sinners?

12 But when Jesus heard *that,* He said unto them, They that are well need not a physician, but they that are sick.

13 But go and learn what *that* meaneth, I will have mercy, and not sacrifice; for I am not come to call the righteous, but sinners to repentance.

Disciples Defended Via Parables
Ezekiel 24:5
Mark 2:18-22
Luke 5:33-39

14 Then came to Him the disciples of John, saying, Why do we and the Pharisees fast often, but thy disciples fast not?

15 And Jesus said unto them, Can the sons of the bridechamber mourn, as long as the bridegroom is with them? But the days will come, when the bridegroom shall be taken from them, and then shall they fast.

16 No man putteth a piece of new cloth on an old garment, for that which is put in to fill it up taketh from the garment, and the tear is made worse.

17 Neither do men put new wine into old wineskins, else the wineskins break, and the wine runneth out, and the wineskins perish; but they put new wine into new wineskins, and both are preserved.

Jairus' Daughter Raised and Woman with Issue of Blood Healed
Mark 5:21-43
Luke 8:40-56

18 While He spoke these things unto them, behold, there came a certain ruler, and worshiped Him, saying, My daughter is even now dead; but come and lay thy hand upon her, and she shall live.
19 And Jesus arose, and followed him, and *so did* His disciples.
20 And, behold, a woman, who had been diseased with an issue of blood twelve years, came behind *Him,* and touched the hem of His garment;
21 For she said within herself, If I may but touch His garment, I shall be well.
22 But Jesus turned about, and when He saw her, He said, Daughter, be of good comfort; thy faith hath made thee well. And the woman was made well from that hour.
23 And when Jesus came into the ruler's house, and saw the musicians and the people making a noise,
24 He said unto them, Give place; for the maid is not dead, but sleepeth. And they laughed Him to scorn.
25 But when the people were put forth, He went in, and took her by the hand, and the maid arose.
26 And the fame of this went abroad into all that land.

Two Blind Men's Sight Restored
27 And when Jesus departed from there, two blind men followed Him, crying, and saying, Thou Son of David, have mercy on us.
28 And when He was come into the house, the blind men came to Him; and Jesus saith unto them, Believe ye that I am able to do this? They said unto Him, Yea, Lord.

29 Then touched He their eyes, saying, According to your faith be it unto you.
30 And their eyes were opened; and Jesus strictly charged them, saying, See *that* no man know *it.*
31 But they, when they were departed, spread abroad His fame in all that country.

Demon Possessed Man Healed
32 As they went out, behold, they brought to Him a dumb man possessed with a demon.
33 And when the demon was cast out, the dumb spoke; and the multitudes marveled, saying, It was never so seen in Israel.
34 But the Pharisees said, He casteth out demons through the prince of the demons.

Twelve Sent Forth
Mark 6:6-13
Luke 9:1-6
I Cor. 9:14

35 And Jesus went about all the cities and villages, teaching in their synagogues, and preaching the gospel of the kingdom, and healing every sickness and every disease among the people.
36 But when He saw the multitudes, He was moved with compassion on them, because they were faint, and were scattered abroad, as sheep having no shepherd.
37 Then saith He unto His disciples, The harvest truly *is* plenteous, but the laborers *are* few.
38 Pray ye, therefore, the Lord of the harvest, that He will send forth laborers into His harvest.

CHAPTER 10

1 And when He had called unto *Him* His twelve disciples, He gave them power *against* unclean spirits, to cast them out, and to heal all manner of sickness and all manner of disease.

PAST	PRESENT	RAPTURE	FIRST 3½ LAST 3½ TRIBULATION		ARMA-GEDDON	MIL-LENNIUM	NEW HEAVENS & EARTH

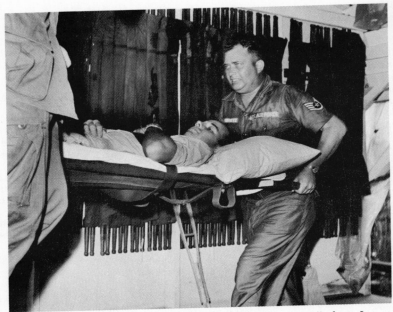

U.S. wounded leaving emergency hospital in Vietnam for flight to Japan.

(Matthew 9:5)

THE PRIORITIES OF GOD

The Pharisees here in Matthew 9:1-8 rejected the sign of the healing miracle, and hardened their hearts in sin. Jesus, realizing their thoughts in verse 5 declares that in Hebrew (Aramaic, the Hebrew of that region) He could have said with less words and effort, "Arise and walk." Yet in order that they should understand that He had the authority from God to forgive sins (and hence, that He was the Christ), He declares that He has made an extra effort to say the longer expression, "Thy sins be forgiven thee." We who love Him respond, "How wonderful;" but they hated Him all the more for this.

Another teaching that could be gleaned from Matthew 9:5 and one that hardly any Christian alive would quarrel with is that the forgiveness of one's sins is even more important than physical healing. Thus even though God can heal in answer to prayer (James 5:14-15), the Gospel ("good news") Message is, "Believe in the Lord Jesus Christ and thou shalt be saved..." **not** "Believe on the Lord Jesus Christ and thou shalt be physically healed."

One way of getting around the high taxes in Israel.

(Matthew 9:12)

TAX COLLECTORS DESPISED

It was the practice in New Testament times to collect tolls on exported goods and custom duties at border towns. Such practice is even in force today. Jesus dined with many tax collectors because He felt their need of Him. Publicans who collected tolls for Rome were the local "tax farmers." They often were assigned a collection quota for their district and they often could keep whatever they received beyond their quotas. The people despised them both because they collected for Rome and because they were notoriously dishonest. Such Publicans are said to have collected about $720,000 a year from Judea and surrounding areas.

Today taxes in threatened Israel—due to their great need for defense funds—are even more exorbitant on some items. If they purchase a car for $3000...their tax on that car is also $3000! And the majority of Israel's money is used for its defense.

Child's body frozen for future

LOS ANGELES (UPI) — A "pretty little French Canadian girl," who died at 8 of cancer, has become the first child to be cryonically frozen to await resurrection attempts when science can deal with the disease.

The Cryonics Society of California identified the child as Genevieve de la Poterie of "a suburb of Montreal," daughter of Guy and Pierette de la Poterie.

She died Tuesday at Children's Hospital, and her body was frozen at a temperature of 275 degrees below zero in liquid nitrogen, said Marshall Neel, a spokesman for the society.

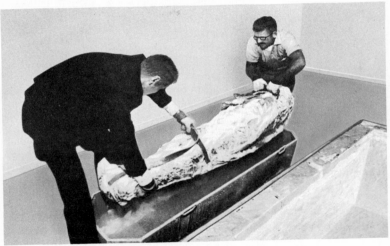

Cryonics Society freeze the dead for future reanimation.

(Matthew 9:20)

WAITING FOR TOMORROW'S MIRACLES

A new society has cropped up in our 20th century. It is the Cryonics Society. This is a movement that freezes the dead for future reanimation, based on the somewhat unsettling prospect that science will one day be able to revive the frozen dead by an electric shock. The group's motto is "Never Say Die." The society now claims membership of over 1000 people. The body is placed in a $4500 cryo-capsule and maintained at a $50 a month expense.

Two children lead a blind man in Jerusalem.

(Matthew 9:28)

GIVING THE BLIND SIGHT

What more precious gift to a blind man is there than to give him his sight! This photograph was taken at the Dome of the Rock in Jerusalem. Here a moslem man is being led to his corner for prayer to Allah by two little children.

What a lesson this is for us. We who know Christ, have our spiritual sight. Yet around us are teeming millions who are blind, spiritually. Let us be as energetic and self-sacrificing as little children in telling them about our precious Saviour. What better way is there to be the "salt of the earth!"

Japanese surrender to General Douglas MacArthur aboard the U.S.S. Missouri in Tokyo Bay on September 2, 1945.

(Matthew 9:37)

TOO LITTLE...FAR TOO LITTLE

General Douglas MacArthur, at the close of World War 2 issued a plea to Americans to flood the country of Japan with missionaries. Only a pitiful handful responded. At that time the doors to Japan were wide open. The people were very receptive.

Now, over a quarter of a century later...less than 1% of the people of Japan call themself "Christian." And an even smaller number are actually born-again Christians who know Christ as personal Saviour and Lord. Japan has shifted to materialism as their god. And Buddhism is their main religion.

(Matthew 10:2)

WHAT IS AN APOSTLE?

The word apostle comes from the Greek **apostolos,** which means "one sent forth." This Greek root, however, differs from other similar words in that it always carries with it the idea, "one sent forth **with a commission,**" that is, with a specified job to be performed. Hence an APOSTLE is one sent forth by the Lord to proclaim the gospel.

As Matthew 10:2-5 shows us, the term **apostle** is first of all applied to the original twelve disciples who were chosen by Christ to be His intimate earthly companions and the primary witnesses to His death and resurrection.

The scriptures, however, also use the word **apostle** in a wider sense beyond the original twelve. Thus Acts 14:14 refers to both Paul and Barnabas as apostles. Indeed in 1 Corinthians 9:1-2 Paul explicitly declares himself to be an apostle on the grounds that he has seen the Lord (on the Damascus Road) and that he was sent to preach the gospel by the Lord Himself. The title is applied to Barnabas apparently because he was explicitly commissioned to preach the gospel by the direct word of the Holy Ghost (Acts 13:1-2). The term is historically not applied to anyone beyond the first century A.D. Thus those saints who lived and wrote in the time of the Lord and immediately after are referred to as the "Apostolic Fathers." Those who lived after that are called, "Church Fathers."

In the days of the apostles special enduement from on high was theirs and they often displayed miraculous signs as the divine credentials showing the truth of the new faith which they proclaimed (Matthew 10:1; Acts 2:1-12; 5:15-16; 16:16-18; 28:3-9).

The fact that **twelve** apostles were picked showed that Christ was establishing a new order which would absorb and replace the former **twelve** tribes. Christ's Church would now transcend the bounds of Israel, and the new twelve would comprehend both Israel and the Gentiles (Matthew 16:18).

In Matthew 19:28 we learn that the original twelve apostles (with Judas replaced) will judge over the twelve tribes of Israel in the coming Kingdom Age. Revelation 21:12-14 shows that in the Eternal state the Holy City, New Jerusalem, will have its twelve gates named for the tribes of Israel, and it will have its huge twelve foundations, between the gates, named for the twelve apostles.

2 Now the names of the twelve apostles are these: the first, Simon, who is called Peter, and Andrew, his brother, James, *the son* of Zebedee, and John, his brother;

3 Philip and Bartholomew; Thomas and Matthew, the tax collector; James, *the son* of Alphaeus, and Lebbaeus, whose surname was Thaddaeus;

4 Simon, the Canaanite, and Judas Iscariot, who also betrayed Him.

5 These twelve Jesus sent forth, and commanded them, saying, Go not into the way of the Gentiles, and into *any* city of the Samaritans enter not;

6 But go, rather, to the lost sheep of the house of Israel.

7 And as ye go, preach, saying, The kingdom of heaven is at hand.

8 Heal the sick, cleanse the lepers, raise the dead, cast out demons; freely ye have received, freely give.

9 Provide neither gold, nor silver, nor copper in your purses,

10 Nor a bag for *your* journey, neither two coats, neither shoes, nor yet a staff; for the workman is worthy of his food.

11 And into whatsoever city or town ye shall enter, inquire who in it is worthy, and there abide till ye go from there.

12 And when ye come into an house, greet it.

13 And if the house be worthy, let your peace come upon it; but if it be not worthy, let your peace return to you.

14 And whosoever shall not receive you, nor hear your words, when ye depart out of that house or city, shake off the dust of your feet.

15 Verily I say unto you, It shall be more tolerable for the land of Sodom and Gomorrah in the day of judgment, than for that city.

16 Behold, I send you forth as sheep in the midst of wolves; be ye, therefore, wise as serpents, and harmless as doves.

17 But beware of men; for they will deliver you up to the councils, and they will scourge you in their synagogues,

18 And ye shall be brought before governors and kings for My sake, for a testimony against them and the Gentiles.

19 But when they deliver you up, be not anxious how or what ye shall speak; for it shall be given you in that same hour what ye shall speak.

20 For it is not ye that speak, but the Spirit of your Father who speaketh in you.

21 And the brother shall deliver up the brother to death, and the father the child; and the children shall rise up against *their* parents, and cause them to be put to death.

22 And ye shall be hated of all *men* for My name's sake, but he that endureth to the end shall be saved.

23 But when they persecute you in this city, flee into another; for verily I say unto you, Ye shall not have gone over the cities of Israel, till the Son of man be come. 1

24 The disciple is not above *his* teacher, nor the servant above his lord.

25 It is enough for the disciple that he be like his teacher, and the servant like his Lord. If they have called the master of the house Beelzebub, how much more *shall they call* them of his household?

26 Fear them not, therefore; for there is nothing covered that shall not be revealed; and hidden, that shall not be known.

27 What I tell you in darkness, *that* speak in light; and what ye hear in the ear, *that* proclaim upon the housetops.

28 And fear not them who kill the body, but are not able to kill the soul; but rather fear him who is able to destroy both soul and body in hell.

---

1 (10:23) A difficult verse with more than one possible interpretation.

29 Are not two sparrows sold for a farthing? And one of them shall not fall on the ground without your Father.

30 But the very hairs of your head are all numbered.

31 Fear not, therefore; ye are of more value than many sparrows.

32 Whosoever, therefore, shall confess Me before men, him will I confess also before My Father, who is in heaven.

33 But whosoever shall deny Me before men, him will I also deny before My Father, who is in heaven.

34 Think not that I am come to send peace on earth; I came not to send peace, but a sword.

35 For I am come to set a man at variance against his father, and the daughter against her mother, and the daughter-in-law against her mother-in-law.

36 And a man's foe *shall be* they of his own household.

37 He that loveth father or mother more than Me, is not worthy of Me; and he that loveth son or daughter more than Me, is not worthy of Me.

38 And he that taketh not his cross and followeth after Me, is not worthy of Me.

39 He that findeth his life shall lose it; and he that loseth his life for My sake shall find it.

40 He that receiveth you receiveth Me, and he that receiveth Me receiveth Him that sent Me.

41 He that receiveth a prophet in the name of a prophet shall receive a prophet's reward; and he that receiveth a righteous man in the name of a righteous man shall receive a righteous man's reward.

42 And whosoever shall give to drink unto one of these little ones a cup of cold *water* only in the name of a disciple, verily I say unto you, he shall in no way lose his reward.

CHAPTER 11

**Jesus Allays
John's Doubts**
● *Galilee*
Luke 7:18-35
Malachi 3:1

1 And it came to pass, when Jesus had ceased commanding His twelve disciples, He departed from there to teach and to preach in their cities.

2 Now, when John had heard in the prison the works of Christ, he sent two of his disciples,

3 And said unto Him, Art thou He that should come, or do we look for another?

4 Jesus answered and said unto them, Go and show John again those things which ye do hear and see:

5 The blind receive their sight, and the lame walk, the lepers are cleansed, and the deaf hear, the dead are raised up, and the poor have the gospel preached to them. 1

6 And blessed is *he,* whosoever shall not be offended in Me.

7 And as they departed, Jesus began to say unto the multitudes concerning John, What went ye out into the wilderness to see? A reed shaken with the wind?

8 But what went ye out to see? A man clothed in soft raiment? Behold, they that wear soft *clothing* are in kings' houses.

9 But what went ye out to see? A prophet? Yea, I say unto you, and more than a prophet.

---

1 (11:5) Christ is leading John to see that He must be the Messiah, because He is even now bringing to pass those things prophesied for the future Messianic Age (the Millennium). (Isaiah 35:5,6; 55:1-4; 61:1.)

PAST	PRESENT	RAPTURE	FIRST 3½ LAST 3½ TRIBULATION	ARMA-GEDDON	MIL-LENNIUM	NEW HEAVENS & EARTH

Photo on left shows members of the Samaritan community offering Passover prayers. Photo on right shows unblemished lamb tied up for sacrifice. There are a little more than 400 Samaritans left...and they all gathered for their Passover ceremony in April, 1972 atop Mount Gerizim in Israel. They ritually slaughtered 13 lambs on what the Samaritans hold to be the site of the Akeda — Abraham's binding of Isaac for sacrifice. The Samaritans live in Nablus and Holon. Following the slaughter, the animals are carried in procession to the altar...some of the blood is sprinkled on the foreheads and white robes of members of the community.

(Matthew 10:5)

A SPECIAL COMMISSION

In these verses we find a special commission given to the apostles. They are told to go at this time to Israel only. In this commission those who they visit will often convey a cordial hospitality to them—but not always. Likewise in the Great Commission the disciples are warned of coming conflicts (Matthew 28:19-20).

Today in Israel, many Jews are still hostile to the things of the Lord. Most have an outward worship, such as at the Wailing Wall, but they deny the Saviour. We who are born again must show them the love of Christ so that they can see that we are not of those who in times past brought persecution to them. Zechariah 12:10 and 8:22-23, in the Old Testament, looks forward to the future conversion and restoration of Israel.

(Matthew 10:14)

MISSIONARIES FACE HARASSMENT IN ISRAEL

News clipping is from the March 17, 1972 issue of THE JERUSALEM POST.

Photo shows Mrs. Sarah Ostrovsky who is manager of the Hebrew Christian bookshop in Jaffa. She is attempting to evict one of the Jewish Defense League members who demonstrated on the premises.

Jewish Defense League members announced that they would continue to "harass" missionaries throughout Israel.

The American Board of Mission to the Jews has also witnessed pressure exerted on their ministry. On Friday, April 2nd, 1971 they planned to televise an hour-long film titled "The Passover." The Synagogue Council of America and the New York Board of Rabbis protested and as a result several television stations refused to sell them program time. Complaints also were issued concerning the American Board's newspaper ad picturing Hebrew Christians.

Will the day of missionary activity in Israel soon come to an end?

J.D.L. PROTEST AGAINST JAFFA 'MISSIONARIES'

The Jewish Defence League's Israel branch has launched a campaign against missionary activity. According to "Yediot Aharonot" reporter Noah Klieger, J.D.L. members, led by their secretary Yosef Schneider, staged a demonstration on Wednesday evening at a bookstore run by the "Hebrew Christians," 42 Rehov Yefet in Jaffa. The shop is managed by Mrs. Sarah Ostrovsky.

The J.D.L. claimed that the "Hebrew Christians" are trying to proselytize immigrants who are staying at a Jewish Agency hostel located in the same building.

After sticking posters on the shop window proclaiming "These are Missionaries," the demonstrators entered the shop, which contains religious literature in many languages, including Russian, English and Spanish. They demanded that Mrs. Ostrovsky cease her "missionary activities." Speaking fluent Hebrew, Mrs. Ostrovsky vehemently denied the charges and tried to evict the young men from her shop.

Finally she called the police, who requested her and three of the demonstrators to go down to headquarters to give evidence.

J.D.L. members announced that they would continue to "harass" missionaries throughout the country.

Israelis test their strength in rope-pulling contest. Their faces picture a determination to endure.

(Matthew 10:22)

THE CHALLENGE TO ENDURE

In Matthew 10:5 to 11:1 we have recorded Jesus' charge to the twelve as He sent them forth to preach the good news of the Kingdom of Heaven. Within this charge to the twelve, in verses 16-23, the Saviour seems to be speaking down the corridors of time, giving a charge to all of His witnesses in every age. Thus here, as in the case of the Great Commission of Matthew 28:18-20, Christ addressed His entire Church represented by the twelve into whose faces He was then gazing.

Matthew 10:22 warns Christians of every age that they will have to endure hatred from the people of this world as a part of their ministry. The world in every age in its majority hates Jesus, and thus it hates those that witness to His name.

Matthew 10:22 further gives a challenge and a promise to the believer in Christ, "...he that endureth to the end shall be saved." Revelation 12:11 tells us how this endurance even unto death comes about...not through the Christian's own strength which would surely fail...but through Christ's atonement for their sins and His enabling and keeping power while they live. Hence, "And they overcame him (Satan) by the blood of the Lamb.."(Revelation 12:11).

American women spend over 2½ BILLION DOLLARS annually to beautify their hair!

(Matthew 10:30)

HAVE YOU COUNTED THE HAIRS ON YOUR HEAD?

Americans are hair-conscious. Each year they spend over $100 million just on hair-coloring preparations...and have a choice of over 180,000 beauty shops where they spend over 2 1/2 BILLION DOLLARS to beautify their hair. In the U.S. alone there are over 500,000 hairdressers.

Yet even though many Christians invest time and money taking care of their hair...they sometimes fail to grasp the fact that Christ is aware of their needs, knows their problems...He even, in fact, knows the very number of the hairs on their head!

1 **10** For this is *he* of whom it is written, Behold, I send My messenger before thy face, who shall prepare thy way before thee.

11 Verily I say unto you, Among them that are born of women there hath not risen a greater than John the Baptist; notwithstanding, he that is least in the kingdom of heaven is greater than he.

12 And from the days of John the Baptist until now the kingdom of heaven suffereth violence, and the violent take it by force.

13 For all the prophets and the law prophesied until John.

2 **14** And if ye will receive *it*, this is Elijah, who was to come.

15 He that hath ears to hear, let him hear.

16 But whereunto shall I liken this generation? It is like unto children sitting in the market places, and calling unto their fellows,

17 And saying, We have piped unto you, and ye have not danced; we have mourned unto you, and ye have not lamented.

18 For John came neither eating nor drinking, and they say, He hath a demon.

19 The Son of man came eating and drinking, and they say, Behold a man gluttonous, and a winebibber, a friend of tax collectors and sinners. But wisdom is justified by her children.

Woes Upon the Privileged
● *Galilee*
Genesis 19:24

20 Then began He to upbraid the cities in which most of His mighty works were done, because they repented not:

21 Woe unto thee, Chorazin! Woe unto thee, Bethsaida! For if the mighty works, which were done in you, had been done in Tyre and Sidon, they would have repented long ago in sackcloth and ashes.

22 But I say unto you, It shall be more tolerable for Tyre and Sidon at the day of judgment, than for you.

23 And thou, Capernaum, which art exalted unto heaven, shalt be brought down to hades; for if the mighty works, which have been done in thee, had been done in Sodom, it would have remained until this day.

24 But I say unto you, That it shall be more tolerable for the land of Sodom in the day of judgment, than for thee.

25 At that time Jesus answered and said, I thank thee, O Father, Lord of heaven and earth, because thou hast hidden these things from the wise and prudent, and hast revealed them unto babes.

26 Even so, Father; for so it seemed good in thy sight.

27 All things are delivered unto Me by My Father, and no man knoweth the Son, but the Father; neither knoweth any man the Father, except the Son, and *he* to whomsoever the Son will reveal *Him*.

28 Come unto Me, all *ye* that labor and are heavy laden, and I will give you rest.

29 Take My yoke upon you, and learn of Me; for I am meek and lowly in heart, and ye shall find rest unto your souls.

30 For My yoke *is* easy, and My burden is light.

CHAPTER 12

Plucked Grain Precipitates Sabbath Controversy
● *En Route to Galilee*
Deut. 5:14
Mark 2:23-28
Luke 6:1-5

1 At that time Jesus went on the sabbath day through the grainfields; and His disciples were hungry, and began to pluck the ears of grain, and to eat.

---

1 (11:10) Behold, I will send My messenger, and he shall prepare the way before Me: and the Lord, whom ye seek, shall suddenly come to His temple, even the messenger of the covenant, whom ye delight in: behold, he shall come, saith the Lord of hosts (Malachi 3:1).

2 (11:14) Behold, I will send you Elijah the prophet before the coming of the great and dreadful day of the Lord (Malachi 4:5).

2 But when the Pharisees saw *it,* they said unto Him, Behold, thy disciples do that which is not lawful to do upon the sabbath day.

3 But He said unto them, Have ye not read what David did, when he was hungry, and they that were with him,

4 How he entered into the house of God, and did eat the showbread, which was not lawful for him to eat, neither for them who were with him, but only for the priests?

5 Or have ye not read in the law, how that on the sabbath days the priests in the temple profane the sabbath, and are blameless?

6 But I say unto you that in this place is *one* greater than the temple.

7 But if ye had known what *this* meaneth, I will have mercy, and not sacrifice, ye would not have condemned the guiltless.

8 For the Son of man is Lord even of the sabbath day.

Withered Hand Healed Causes Another Sabbath Controversy
● *Galilee*
Mark 3:1-6
Luke 6:6-11
Acts 28:8-9

9 And when He was departed from there, He went into their synagogue.

10 And, behold, there was a man who had *his* hand paralyzed. And they asked Him, saying, Is it lawful to heal on the sabbath days? that they might accuse Him.

11 And He said unto them, What man shall there be among you, that shall have one sheep, and if it fall into a pit on the sabbath day, will he not lay hold on it, and lift *it* out?

12 How much, then, is a man better than a sheep? Wherefore, it is lawful to do good on the sabbath days.

13 Then saith He to the man, Stretch forth thine hand. And he stretched *it* forth; and it was restored well like the other.

14 Then the Pharisees went out, and held a council against Him, how they might destroy Him.

Multitudes Healed
● *Sea of Galilee*
Mark 3:7-12
Luke 6:17-19

15 But when Jesus knew *it,* He withdrew Himself from there; and great multitudes followed Him, and He healed them all,

16 And charged them that they should not make Him known,

17 That it might be fulfilled which was spoken by Isaiah, the prophet, saying, 1

18 Behold My servant, whom I have chosen; My beloved, in whom My soul is well pleased; I will put My Spirit upon Him, and He shall show justice to the Gentiles.

19 He shall not strive, nor cry; neither shall any man hear His voice in the streets.

20 A bruised reed shall He not break, and smoking flax shall He not quench, till He send forth justice unto victory.

21 And in His name shall the Gentiles trust.

Jesus Accused of Blasphemy
● *Capernaum*
Mark 3:19-30
Luke 11:14-23

22 Then was brought unto Him one possessed with a demon, blind, and dumb; and He healed him, insomuch that the blind and dumb both spoke and saw.

23 And all the people were amazed, and said, Is not this the son of David? 2

---

1 (12:17) Isaiah 42:1-4.

2 (12:23) This is a Messianic title referring to the Christ, the final Son of David. Jeremiah 23:5-8; Isaiah 11:1,9 (Jesse was David's father).

PAST	PRESENT	RAPTURE	FIRST 3½ TRIBULATION	LAST 3½	ARMA-GEDDON	MIL-LENNIUM	NEW HEAVENS & EARTH

Ruins at Chorazin, presumably remains of a synagogue.

(Matthew 11:21)

CHORAZIN ANNIHILATED

Jesus pronounced God's sentence of annihilation upon whole towns such as Chorazin, Bethsaida and Capernaum because they had rejected His call to repentance.

The ruins of Chorazin are about 2 miles north of Capernaum. Chorazin must have at one time been an important city, but now only a few stones remain. Even the boundaries of Capernaum are still in dispute. Will such judgments fall on New York City and Los Angeles because of their lustful material depravity?

Children look in awe at Hasidic (orthodox) Jew in Jerusalem.

(Matthew 11:29)

UNDERSTANDING GOD'S YOKE

Yoke has several meanings. In primitive agriculture a yoke was a piece of curved timber fitted with bows for the necks to control animals as they pulled a plow. It is a weight and a yoke of slavery.

Christ here is speaking of a form of spiritual slavery. He refers to the Jews who bear the "yoke of the law," the legalistic rabbinical piety that weighed heavily on their daily walk. Using this as an example, He invites the seeking one to take His yoke, "the yoke of the Kingdom." For in so doing they will find His yoke easy, His burden light. The Yoke of the Pharisees produced slavery. The yoke of God provides freedom and eternal life.

Which yoke are you bearing?

24 But when the Pharisees heard *it,* they said, This *fellow* doth not cast out demons, but by Beelzebub, the prince of the demons.

25 And Jesus knew their thoughts, and said unto them, Every kingdom divided against itself is brought to desolation; and every city or house divided against itself shall not stand.

26 And if Satan cast out Satan, he is divided against himself; how shall then his kingdom stand?

27 And if I, by Beelzebub, cast out demons, by whom do your sons cast *them* out? Therefore, they shall be your judges.

28 But if I cast out demons by the Spirit of God, then the kingdom of God is come unto you.

29 Or else how can one enter into a strong man's house, and spoil his goods, except he first bind the strong man? And then he will spoil his house.

30 He that is not with Me is against Me; and he that gathereth not with Me scattereth abroad.

31 Wherefore, I say unto you, All manner of sin and blasphemy shall be forgiven men; but the blasphemy *against* the *Holy* Spirit shall not be forgiven men.

32 And whosoever speaketh a word against the Son of man, it shall be forgiven him; but whosoever speaketh against the Holy Spirit, it shall not be forgiven him, neither in this age, neither in the *age* to come.

33 Either make the tree good, and its fruit good, or else make the tree corrupt, and its fruit corrupt; for the tree is known by *its* fruit.

34 O generation of vipers, how can ye, being evil, speak good things? For out of the abundance of the heart the mouth speaketh.

35 A good man out of the good treasure of the heart bringeth forth good things, and an evil man out of the evil treasure bringeth forth evil things.

36 But I say unto you that every idle word that men shall speak, they shall give account of it in the day of judgment. [1]

37 For by thy words thou shalt be justified, and by thy words thou shalt be condemned.

**Jesus' Answer to Demand
For a Sign**
● *Capernaum*
Luke 11:24-26, 29-36

38 Then certain of the scribes and of the Pharisees answered, saying, Master, we would see a sign from thee.

39 But He answered and said unto them, An evil and adulterous generation seeketh after a sign, and there shall no sign be given to it, but the sign of the prophet, Jonah;

40 For as Jonah was three days and three nights in the belly of the great fish, so shall the Son of man be three days and three nights in the heart of the earth.

41 The men of Nineveh shall rise in judgment with this generation, and shall condemn it; because they repented at the preaching of Jonah; and, behold, a greater than Jonah *is* here.

42 The queen of the south shall rise up in the judgment with this generation, and shall condemn it; for she came from the farthest parts of the earth to hear the wisdom of Solomon; and, behold, a greater than Solomon *is* here.

43 When the unclean spirit is gone out of a man, he walketh through dry places, seeking rest, and findeth none.

44 Then he saith, I will return into my house from which I came out; and when he is come, he findeth *it* empty, swept, and garnished.

1 (12:36) Christ here views all of the coming judgments as one, such as, the Judgment Seat of Christ after the Rapture and the Great White Throne.

1 45 Then goeth he, and taketh with himself seven other spirits more wicked than himself, and they enter in and dwell there; and the last *state* of that man is worse than the first. Even so shall it be also unto this wicked generation.

**Mother, Brother
Seek Audience**
• *Capernaum*
Mark 3:31-35
Luke 8:19-21

46 While He yet talked to the people, behold, *His* mother and His brethren stood outside, desiring to speak with Him.
47 Then one said unto Him, Behold, thy mother and thy brethren stand outside, desiring to speak with thee.
48 But He answered and said unto him that told Him, Who is My mother? And who are My brethren?
49 And He stretched forth His hand toward His disciples, and said, Behold My mother and My brethren!
50 For whosoever shall do the will of My Father, who is in heaven, the same is My brother, and sister, and mother.

CHAPTER 13

• *By Sea of Galilee*
Mark 4:1-34
Luke 8:4-18
Joel 3:13

1 The same day went Jesus out of the house, and sat by the seaside.

2 And great multitudes were gathered together unto Him, so that He went into a boat, and sat; and the whole multitude stood on the shore.

Parable of Sower

3 And He spoke many things unto them in parables, saying, Behold, a sower went forth to sow;
4 And when he sowed, some *of the seeds* fell by the wayside, and the fowls came and devoured them.
5 Some fell upon stony places, where they had not much earth; and forthwith they sprang up, because they had no deepness of earth.
6 And when the sun was up, they were scorched; and because they had no root, they withered away.
7 And some fell among thorns; and the thorns sprang up, and choked them.
8 But other *seeds* fell into good ground, and brought forth fruit, some an hundredfold, some sixtyfold, some thirtyfold.
9 Who hath ears to hear, let him hear.
10 And the disciples came, and said unto Him, Why speakest thou unto them in parables?
11 He answered and said unto them, Because it is given unto you to know the mysteries of the kingdom of heaven, but to them it is not given.
12 For whosoever hath, to him shall be given, and he shall have more abundance; but whosoever hath not, from him shall be taken away even what he hath.
13 Therefore speak I to them in parables, because they seeing, see not; and hearing, they hear not, neither do they understand.

1 (12:45) Rejecting certain external sins (the first unclean spirit), the Pharisees would not fill themselves with Christ and God's righteousness. Thus worse sins entered and filled the empty space.

PAST	PRESENT	RAPTURE	FIRST 3½	LAST 3½	ARMA-GEDDON	MIL-LENNIUM	NEW HEAVENS & EARTH
			TRIBULATION				

MODERN DAY HOLY COMMUNION

In Dallas, Texas...ADVENT...(the coming of Christ and the period including the 4 Sundays before Christmas)...was celebrated by a worshiper in hot pants dancing down the aisles after HOLY COMMUNION. She was joined by the Chaplain of Perkins Chapel.

This occurred at Southern Methodist University. The congregation was given crepe paper stoles and streamers. The dancing at the service was part of the Chaplain's program to relate religion to today's youth.

Satanic baptism at Church of Satan in Los Angeles.

(Matthew 12:31)

WHAT IS THE UNPARDONABLE SIN?

In verse 31 we find that the unpardonable sin is the blasphemy against the Holy Spirit. The Pharisees continually denied the truth that the miracles of Jesus represented the power of God. They ascribed these miracles to the devil. See Matthew 23:13-36.

Thus from its context it would seem that the unpardonable sin is a final decision of the heart whereby a sinner who sees the work of God's Holy Spirit says a final and determined, "No." The sinner wilfully blasphemes the Holy Spirit by attributing His works to evil. By this final decision the sinner forever banishes the Holy Spirit from dealing further with him, and hence he is irretrievably lost forever. Thus the sin is unpardonable.

Today one can find in Los Angeles the Church of Satan, as well as many who turn to astrology, to mysticism and who constantly blaspheme the deity of God.

(Matthew 12:39)

THE SIGN OF PEACE

In the early 1970's the peace sign became a familiar symbol. Many believe it is Satanically inspired. One fact remains. Young people, fed up with the hypocrisy of those around them...their striving for material gains...their involvement in multiple wars...were desperately seeking an answer.

Unfortunately, many looked in the wrong direction. They clung to the peace symbol hoping that peace would finally come to mankind. But they sought peace without seeking the King of Peace...the Lord Jesus Christ.

Antiwar protester flings his medals towards Capitol at Washington "peace" rally in April, 1971. Vietnam veteran joins others at U.S. capital in discarding military decorations.

(Matthew 12:42)

ENTER THE QUEEN OF SHEBA

It was probably from Arabia that Solomon mined the gold and precious stones of "Ophir;" also it was probably from South Arabia that the Queen of Sheba came to seek his friendship and perhaps his aid. We are told that the "weight of gold that came to Solomon in one year was 626 talents of gold." It has been estimated that a talent in today's market would have a purchasing power of $10,000. If this is so, in one year Solomon received over $6 MILLION in gold.

The Queen of Sheba came from a far country to hear the wisdom of Solomon...

> Yet people will not be persuaded to come and hear the wisdom of   Christ.

The Queen of Sheba had no invitation to come to Solomon, nor any promise of being welcome...

> But we are invited to Christ, to sit at His feet and hear His Word.

The Queen of Sheba could not be sure that it would be worth her while to go so far on this errand...

> But we come to Christ without such uncertainties!

The Queen of Sheba came from the uttermost parts of the earth (verse 42)...

> But we have Christ among us. Behold, He stands at the door, and knocks! (Revelation 3:20)

The Archbishop of Canterbury stands to the Queen's right, having just placed the Crown on the head of Queen Elizabeth II during her coronation in 1952.

FLYING SAUCER?
A housewife in Oregon was out taking pictures when this object came into her camera view. A flying saucer? No one knows. All are agreed it is a "mystery." Perhaps time will reveal what this phenomena is.

(Matthew 13:11)
UNRAVELLING A MYSTERY
In Scriptures, a "mystery" is a previously hidden truth which is now divinely revealed. In the Old Testament many mysteries were only hinted at or kept secret because the mystery was too profound for the human mind to fully grasp at that stage in God's revealing His Divine plans. Now after the cross, we are able to comprehend a few more of these mysteries.

In the Greco-Roman mystery religions, the mysteries were the **secrets** which only the initiated members of the group knew. Now we who trust Christ, through the words of the Bible and the illumination of the Holy Spirit, are being shown the mysteries of our religion.

Chapter 13 of Matthew shows clearly for the first time in an unmistakable way that there will be an interval between Christ's first coming and His Second Coming. The word "mystery" occurs some 27 times in the New Testament. In many cases it refers to the plan of salvation or some aspect thereof.

UNI-SEX

(Matthew 13:38)

THE SEED AND TARES OF TODAY'S WORLD

The 1970's introduced a new word—UNISEX. This blurring of masculine and feminine distinctions has become another product of this permissive age. The crisscrossing of appearances has gone so far that certain stylish boutiques now sell unisex outfits that can be worn by either man or women.

Perhaps this is a modern day illustration of the seed and tares. At quick glance they cannot be told apart. But when the harvest comes, the true wheat will be fruitful, the tares will suffer the wrath of the reaper.

How important it is for Christians not to blend in with worldly trends... to be **in** the world...but not to be **of** the world. This increasingly is becoming a challenge as many churches compromise their message and their standards.

1 14 And in them is fulfilled the prophecy of Isaiah, which saith, By hearing, ye shall hear and shall not understand; and seeing, ye shall see and shall not perceive;
15 For this people's heart is become gross, and *their* ears are dull of hearing, and their eyes they have closed, lest at any time they should see with *their* eyes, and hear with *their* ears, and should understand with *their* heart, and should be converted, and I should heal them.
16 But blessed *are* your eyes, for they see; and your ears, for they hear.
17 For verily I say unto you that many prophets and righteous *men* have desired to see *those things* which ye see, and have not seen *them;* and to hear *those things* which ye hear, and have not heard *them.*

Parable Interpreted
18 Hear, therefore, the parable of the sower.
19 When any one heareth the word of the kingdom, and understandeth *it* not, then cometh the wicked *one,* and catcheth away that which was sown in his heart. This is he which received seed by the wayside.
20 But he that received the seed in stony places, the same is he that heareth the word, and immediately with joy receiveth it;
21 Yet hath he not root in himself, but endureth for a while; for when tribulation or persecution ariseth because of the word, immediately he is offended.

22 He also that received seed among the thorns is he that heareth the word; and the care of this age, and the deceitfulness of riches, choke the word, and he becometh unfruitful.
23 But he that received seed in the good ground is he that heareth the word, and understandeth *it,* who also beareth fruit, and bringeth forth, some an hundredfold, some sixty, some thirty.

Parable of Tares
24 Another parable put He forth unto them, saying, The kingdom of heaven is likened unto a man who sowed good seed in his field;
25 But, while men slept, his enemy came and sowed tares among the wheat, and went his way.
26 But when the blade was sprung up, and brought forth fruit, then appeared the tares also.
27 So the servants of the householder came and said unto him, Sir, didst not thou sow good seed in thy field? From where, then, hath it tares?
28 He said unto them, An enemy hath done this. The servants said unto him, Wilt thou, then, that we go and gather them up?
29 But he said, Nay; lest while ye gather up the tares, ye root up also the wheat with them.
30 Let both grow together until the harvest; and in the time of harvest I will say to the reapers, Gather together first the tares, and bind them in bundles to burn them, but gather the wheat into my barn. 2

1 (13:14-15) And He said, Go, and tell this people, Hear ye indeed, but understand not; and see ye indeed, but perceive not.
Make the heart of this people fat, and make their ears heavy, and shut their eyes; lest they see with their eyes, and hear with their ears, and understand with their heart, and convert, and be healed (Isaiah 6:9, 10).

2 (13:30-43) Here and also in the judgments described in the following verses the Rapture, Armageddon, and the Great White Throne Judgment are all seen together.

Parable of Mustard Seed

31 Another parable put He forth unto them, saying, The kingdom of heaven is like a grain of mustard seed, which a man took, and sowed in his field;

32 Which, indeed, is the least of all seeds; but when it is grown, it is the greatest among herbs, and becometh a tree, so that the birds of the air come and lodge in the branches of it.

Parable of Leaven

33 Another parable spoke He unto them, *saying,* The kingdom of heaven is like leaven, which a woman took, and hid in three measures of meal, till the whole was leavened.

34 All these things spoke Jesus unto the multitude in parables, and without a parable spoke He not unto them,

35 That it might be fulfilled which was spoken by the prophet, saying, I will open My mouth in parables; I will utter things which have been kept secret from the foundation of the world.

36 Then Jesus sent the multitude away, and went into the house; and His disciples came unto Him, saying, Explain unto us the parable of the tares of the field.

37 He answered and said unto them, He that soweth the good seed is the Son of man;

38 The field is the world; the good seed are the children of the kingdom, but the tares are the children of the wicked *one;*

39 The enemy that sowed them is the devil; the harvest is the end of the age; and the reapers are the angels.

40 As, therefore, the tares are gathered and burned in the fire, so shall it be in the end of this age.

41 The Son of man shall send forth His angels, and they shall gather out of His kingdom all things that offend, and them who do iniquity,

42 And shall cast them into a furnace of fire; there shall be wailing and gnashing of teeth.

43 Then shall the righteous shine forth as the sun in the kingdom of their Father. Who hath ears to hear, let him hear.

Parable of Hid Treasure

44 Again, the kingdom of heaven is like treasure hidden in a field, which when a man hath found, he hideth, and for joy of it goeth and selleth all that he hath, and buyeth that field.

Parable of the Pearl

45 Again, the kingdom of heaven is like a merchant man, seeking fine pearls,

46 Who, when he had found one pearl of great price, went and sold all that he had, and bought it.

Parable of the Net

47 Again, the kingdom of heaven is like a net, that was cast into the sea, and gathered of every kind,

48 Which, when it was full, they drew to shore, and sat down, and gathered the good into vessels, but cast the bad away.

49 So shall it be at the end of the age; the angels shall come forth, and separate the wicked from among the righteous, [1]

50 And shall cast them into the furnace of fire; there shall be wailing and gnashing of teeth.

51 Jesus saith unto them, Have ye understood all these things? They say unto Him, Yea, Lord.

---

1 (13:49-50) Here again the Rapture, Armageddon, and the Great White Throne Judgment are all seen together.

PAST	PRESENT	RAPTURE	FIRST 3½ LAST 3½ TRIBULATION		ARMA-GEDDON	MIL-LENNIUM	NEW HEAVENS & EARTH

Wilburn Dowell Cobb holds the Pearl of Allah, a 14 pound gem he sold for $3.5 million. For more than two decades he kept it in bank vaults and museums.

(Matthew 13:45)

"PRESSED FOR TIME"

In 1934 Dwak natives on the island of Palawan near the Philippines found a great pearl. It weighed 14 pounds, 1 ounce. Wilburn D. Cobb said he received this pearl as a gift for curing the Philippine chief's son of malaria.

In 1969 Cobb sold this giant pearl for $3.5 million because, as he stated, "I'm pressed for time. I'm 65 years old." He plans to use the money to buy a plantation for the natives who found the pearl.

Many commentators feel that the pearl of great price is Christ Himself and the salvation which is offered in Him. He is worth the leaving of everything else. Others, however, suggest that the true Church is the pearl of great price. Christ, having given Himself for the pearl, is now preparing it for presentation to Himself. See Ephesians 5:25-27.

Nazareth as it looks today. Motion picture theater is focal point of entertainment in town.

(Matthew 13:57)

WITHOUT HONOR IN HIS OWN COUNTRY

Even though He was known as "Jesus of Nazareth" in Nazareth Christ was rejected (Acts 2:22).

How true this is even today. Those who have achieved some accomplishment are sought out for recognition, in many instances, everywhere except in their own hometown.

Nazareth today is simply a small, unpretentious town. Nothing much seems to be going on there except for the periodic visit of some tourists. It lost its opportunity for greatness because it did not recognize a prophet. In this case, it failed to honor the Lord Jesus Christ.

Yet let us not shed all of our pity and sorrow on Nazareth. How many Nazareths are found in the homes of your relatives, your friends...in your own home? Has your family honored Jesus?

Parable of Householder

52 Then said He unto them, Therefore, every scribe *who is* instructed concerning the kingdom of heaven is like a man *that is* an householder, who bringeth forth out of his treasure *things* new and old.

Nazareth's 2nd Rejection of Christ

● *Nazareth*
Mark 6:1-6

53 And it came to pass *that,* when Jesus had finished these parables, He departed from there.

1   54 And when He was come into His own country, He taught them in their synagogue, insomuch that they were astonished, and said, From where hath this *man* this wisdom, and *these* mighty works?

55 Is not this the carpenter's son? Is not His mother called Mary? And His brethren, James, and Joseph, and Simon, and Judas?

56 And His sisters, are they not all with us? From where, then, hath this *man* all these things?

57 And they were offended in Him. But Jesus said unto them, A prophet is not without honor, except in his own country, and in his own house.

58 And He did not many mighty works there because of their unbelief.

CHAPTER 14

Fearful Herod Beheads John

Spring 29 A.D.
● *Galilee*
Mark 6:14-29
Luke 9:7-9

1 At that time Herod, the tetrarch, heard of the fame of Jesus,

2 And said unto his servants, This is John the Baptist; he is risen from the dead, and therefore mighty works do show forth themselves in him.

3 For Herod had laid hold on John, and bound him, and put *him* in prison for Herodias' sake, his brother Philip's wife.

4 For John said unto him, It is not lawful for thee to have her.

5 And when he would have put him to death, he feared the multitude, because they counted him as a prophet.

6 But when Herod's birthday was kept, the daughter of Herodias danced before them, and pleased Herod.

7 Whereupon he promised with an oath to give her whatsoever she would ask.

8 And she, being before instructed of her mother, said, Give me here the head of John the Baptist on a platter.

9 And the king was sorry; nevertheless, for the oath's sake, and them who sat dining with him, he commanded *it* to be given *her.*

10 And he sent, and beheaded John in the prison.

11 And his head was brought on a platter and given to the girl, and she brought *it* to her mother.

12 And his disciples came, and took up the body, and buried it, and went and told Jesus.

Return of the Twelve
Jesus Retires; 5000 Fed

● *Near Bethsaida*
Mark 6:30-44
Luke 9:10-17
John 6:1-14

13 When Jesus heard *of it,* He departed from there by boat into a desert place privately; and when the people had heard *of it,* they followed Him on foot out of the cities.

14 And Jesus went forth, and saw a great multitude, and was moved with compassion toward them, and He healed their sick.

15 And when it was evening, His disciples came to Him, saying, This is a desert place, and the time is now late; send the multitude away, that they may go into the villages, and buy themselves food.

---

1   (13:54-58) Luke 4:16-30 tells of the first Nazareth visitation.

16 But Jesus said unto them, They need not depart; give them to eat.

17 And they say unto Him, We have here but five loaves, and two fishes.

18 He said, Bring them here to Me.

19 And He commanded the multitude to sit down on the grass, and took the five loaves, and the two fishes, and looking up to heaven, He blessed, and broke, and gave the loaves to *His* disciples, and the disciples *gave them* to the multitude.

20 And they did all eat, and were filled; and they took up of the fragments that remained twelve baskets full.

21 And they that had eaten were about five thousand men, besides women and children.

Jesus Walks on the Water
Mark 6:45-52
John 6:16-21

22 And straightway Jesus constrained His disciples to get into a boat, and to go before Him unto the other side, while He sent the multitudes away.

23 And when He had sent the multitudes away, He went up into a mountain privately, to pray; and when the evening was come, He was there alone.

24 But the boat was now in the midst of the sea, tossed with waves; for the wind was contrary.

25 And in the fourth watch of the night Jesus went unto them, walking on the sea.

26 And when the disciples saw Him walking on the sea, they were troubled, saying, It is a ghost; and they cried out for fear.

27 But straightway Jesus spoke unto them, saying, Be of good cheer; it is I; be not afraid.

28 And Peter answered Him and said, Lord, if it be thou, bid me come unto thee on the water.

29 And He said, Come. And when Peter was come down out of the boat, he walked on the water, to go to Jesus.

30 But when he saw the wind boisterous, he was afraid; and beginning to sink, he cried, saying, Lord, save me.

31 And immediately Jesus stretched forth *His* hand, and caught him, and said unto him, O thou of little faith, why didst thou doubt?

32 And when they were come into the boat, the wind ceased.

33 Then they that were in the boat came and worshiped Him, saying, Of a truth, thou art the Son of God.

The Sick Healed
● *Gennesaret*
Mark 6:53-56

34 And when they were gone over, they came into the land of Gennesaret.

35 And when the men of that place had knowledge of Him, they sent out into all that country round about, and brought unto Him all that were diseased.

36 And besought Him that they might only touch the hem of His garment; and as many as touched were made perfectly well.

CHAPTER 15
Traditions Attacked
29 A.D.
Mark 7:1-23
John 7:1

1 Then came to Jesus scribes and Pharisees, who were of Jerusalem, saying,

2 Why do thy disciples transgress the tradition of the elders? For they wash not their hands when they eat bread.

3 But He answered and said unto them, Why do ye also transgress the commandment of God by your tradition?

4 For God commanded, saying, Honor thy father and mother; and, He that curseth father or mother, let him die the death.

PAST	PRESENT	RAPTURE	FIRST 3½	LAST 3½	ARMA-GEDDON	MIL-LENNIUM	NEW HEAVENS & EARTH
			TRIBULATION				

Dawn gets ready for first day at school.

Brother Duane provides reassuring arm. *First step in tomorrow's world.*

(Matthew 14:31)

FAITH WITHOUT FALTERING

Peter took a step of faith. In the midst of what seemed an impossibility, he walked upon the water. He did so because Jesus said, "Come." Then Peter apparently saw the white caps and wind boisterous... and his faith faltered. While he first seemed to say, Lord I believe...suddenly his plea became Lord, help my unbelief. With his faith faltering... he begins to sink.

Christ replies, "Why didst thou doubt?" What a lesson for us today. Many missionaries have the faith to step onto foreign shores. What if suddenly when they see the winds of adversity around them, their faith should falter and they should return home? Many Christians at home have faith on Sunday but sink into the ocean of doubt all the rest of the week. If Christ is Lord **at** all, He must be Lord **of** all!

(Matthew 15:28)
LORD, HELP ME!

How often have you actually prayed this prayer? I have many times. And each time the Lord has answered...oftentimes with some day by day miracle I would never have expected. Sometimes one has to be at the "end of the rope" before in desperation he turns to God. Actually, when a need arises...your first thought should be to bring the request to God. The simple prayer of LORD, HELP ME can open up avenues of untold blessings in your life.

The woman of Canaan in verse 22 was at "wit's end corner." And it appeared that even the doors of Heaven were shut to her. But Jesus, touched by her faith...quickly answered her prayer for the healing of her daughter. Are there real problems in your life? Have you tried seeking God's guidance and direction?

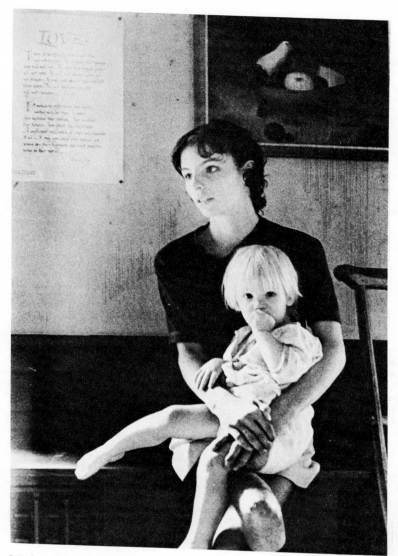

Mother's Last Thoughts

Mrs. Lyn Helton, who suffers from an incurable disease called osteosarcoma that would soon kill her, sits reflecting with her 20-month-old daughter, Jennifer. A thief, hours before, sneaked into their home and stole the tape recording on thoughts about death Mrs. Helton was making to be used in a research project. (Mrs. Helton died a few short months after this photograph was taken.)

5 But ye say, Whosoever shall say to *his* father or *his* mother, *It is* a gift, by whatsoever thou mightest be profited by me;

6 And honor not his father or his mother, *he shall be free.* Thus have ye made the commandment of God of no effect by your tradition.

[1] 7 Ye hypocrites, well did Isaiah prophesy of you, saying,

8 This people draweth near unto Me with their mouth, and honoreth Me with *their* lips, but their heart is far from Me.

9 But in vain they do worship Me, teaching *for* doctrines the commandments of men.

10 And He called the multitude, and said unto them, Hear, and understand:

11 Not that which goeth into the mouth defileth a man, but that which cometh out of the mouth, this defileth a man.

12 Then came His disciples, and said unto Him, Knowest thou that the Pharisees were offended, after they heard this saying?

13 But He answered and said, Every plant, which My heavenly Father hath not planted, shall be rooted up.

14 Let them alone; they are blind leaders of the blind. And if the blind lead the blind, both shall fall into the ditch.

15 Then answered Peter and said unto Him, Explain unto us this parable.

16 And Jesus said, Are ye also yet without understanding?

17 Do not ye yet understand, that whatsoever entereth in at the mouth goeth into the stomach, and is cast out into the draught?

18 But those things which proceed out of the mouth come forth from the heart, and they defile the man.

19 For out of the heart proceed evil thoughts, murders, adulteries, for-

nications, thefts, false witness, blasphemies.

20 These are *the things* which defile a man; but to eat with unwashed hands defileth not a man.

Healing of Syrophenician Woman
● *Phoenicia*
Mark 7:24-30

21 Then Jesus went from there, and departed into the borders of Tyre and Sidon.

22 And, behold, a woman of Canaan came out of the same borders, and cried unto Him, saying, Have mercy on me, O Lord, *thou* Son of David; my daughter is grievously vexed with a demon.

23 But He answered her not a word. And His disciples came and besought Him, saying, Send her away; for she crieth after us.

24 But He answered and said, I am not sent but unto the lost sheep of the house of Israel.

25 Then came she and worshiped Him, saying, Lord, help me.

26 But He answered and said, It is not right to take the children's bread, and to cast *it* to dogs.

27 And she said, Truth, Lord; yet the dogs eat of the crumbs which fall from their master's table.

28 Then Jesus answered and said unto her, O woman, great *is* thy faith; be it unto thee even as thou wilt. And her daughter was made well from that very hour.

Afflicted Healed
● *Decapolis*
Mark 7:31-37

29 And Jesus departed from there, and came near unto the Sea of Galilee, and went up into a mountain, and sat down there.

---

1 (15:7-9) Wherefore the Lord said, Forasmuch as this people draw near Me with their mouth, and with their lips do honour Me, but have removed their heart far from Me, and their fear toward Me is taught by the precept of men (Isaiah 29:13).

1 30 And great multitudes came unto Him, having with them *those that were* lame, blind, dumb, maimed, and many others, and put them down at Jesus' feet; and He healed them,
31 Insomuch that the multitude wondered, when they saw the dumb to speak, the maimed to be well, the lame to walk, and the blind to see; and they glorified the God of Israel.

4000 Fed
● *Decapolis*
Mark 8:1-9

32 Then Jesus called His disciples *unto Him*, and said, I have compassion on the multitude, because they continue with Me now three days, and have nothing to eat; and I will not send them away fasting, lest they faint in the way.
33 And His disciples say unto Him, From where should we have so much bread in the wilderness, as to fill so great a multitude?
34 And Jesus saith unto them, How many loaves have ye? And they said, Seven, and a few little fishes.
35 And He commanded the multitude to sit down on the ground.
36 And He took the seven loaves and the fishes, and gave thanks, and broke *them*, and gave to His disciples, and the disciples to the multitude.
37 And they did all eat, and were filled: and they took up of the broken pieces that were left seven baskets full.
38 And they that did eat were four thousand men, besides women and children.

39 And He sent away the multitude, and got into a boat and came into the borders of Magadan.

CHAPTER 16

The Pharisees Require a Sign
● *Magdala*
Mark 8:10-13

1 The Pharisees, with the Sadducees, came and, testing Him, desired that He would show them a sign from heaven.
2 He answered and said unto them, When it is evening, ye say, *It will be* fair weather; for the sky is red.
3 And in the morning, *It will be* foul weather today; for the sky is red and overcast. O *ye* hypocrites, ye can discern the face of the sky; but can ye not *discern* the signs of the times?

Sign Seekers Rebuked
2 4 A wicked and adulterous generation seeketh after a sign; and there shall no sign be given unto it, but the sign of the prophet, Jonah. And He left them, and departed.

5 And when His disciples were come to the other side, they had forgotten to take bread.

Warning on False Doctrine
Mark 8:14-26

6 Then Jesus said unto them, Take heed and beware of the leaven of the Pharisees and of the Sadducees.
7 And they reasoned among themselves, saying, *It is* because we have taken no bread,

---

1 (15:30-31) Then the eyes of the blind shall be opened, and the ears of the deaf shall be unstopped.

Then shall the lame man leap as an hart, and the tongue of the dumb sing: for in the wilderness shall waters break out, and streams in the desert (Isaiah 35:5-6).

2 (16:4) His fulfillment of Messianic prophecy and His holy life were not enough for these sinners; they wanted Him to show a "magic trick." There would, however, yet be the sign of Jonah for that generation — His resurrection (Matthew 12:40).

PAST	PRESENT	RAPTURE	FIRST 3½ LAST 3½ TRIBULATION		ARMA-GEDDON	MIL-LENNIUM	NEW HEAVENS & EARTH

8 *Which,* when Jesus perceived, He said unto them, O ye of little faith, why reason ye among yourselves, because ye have brought no bread?

9 Do ye not yet understand, neither remember the five loaves of the five thousand, and how many baskets ye took up?

10 Neither the seven loaves of the four thousand, and how many baskets ye took up?

11 How is it that ye do not understand that I spoke not to you concerning bread, *but* that ye should beware of the leaven of the Pharisees and of the Sadducees?

12 Then understood they that He bade *them* not *to* beware of the leaven of bread, but of the doctrine of the Pharisees and of the Sadducees.

Peter Confesses Jesus is Christ
● *Near Caesarea Philippi*
Mark 8:27-30
Luke 9:18-21

13 When Jesus came into the borders of Caesarea Philippi, He asked His disciples, saying, Who do men say that I, the Son of man, am?

1 14 And they said, Some *say that thou art* John the Baptist; some, Elijah; and others, Jeremiah, or one of the prophets.

15 He saith unto them, But who say ye that I am?

16 And Simon Peter answered and said, Thou art the Christ, the Son of the living God.

17 And Jesus answered and said unto him, Blessed art thou, Simon Barjona; for flesh and blood hath not revealed *it* unto thee, but My Father, who is in heaven.

18 And I say also unto thee, That 2 thou art Peter, and upon this rock I will build My church, and the gates of hades shall not prevail against it.

19 And I will give unto thee the keys 3 of the kingdom of heaven; and whatsoever thou shalt bind on earth shall be bound in heaven; and whatsoever thou shalt loose on earth shall be loosed in heaven.

20 Then charged He His disciples that they should tell no man that He was Jesus, the Christ.

**Jesus Foretells His Death
and Resurrection**
● *Caesarea Philippi*
Mark 8:31-37
Luke 9:22-25

21 From that time forth began Jesus to show unto His disciples, how He must go unto Jerusalem, and suffer many things from the elders and chief priests and scribes, and be killed, and be raised again the third day.

22 Then Peter took Him, and began to rebuke Him, saying, Be it far from thee, Lord; this shall not be unto thee.

23 But He turned and said unto Peter, Get thee behind Me, Satan. Thou art an offense unto Me; for thou savorest not the things that are of God, but those that are of men.

1 (16:14) I will raise them up a prophet from among their brethren, like unto thee, and will put My words in his mouth; and he shall speak unto them all that I shall command him.

And it shall come to pass, that whosoever will not hearken unto My words which he shall speak in My name, I will require it of him (Deuteronomy 18:18-19).

Behold, I will send you Elijah the prophet before the coming of the great and dreadful day of the Lord:

And he shall turn the heart of the fathers to the children, and the heart of the children to their fathers, lest I come and smite the earth with a curse (Malachi 4:5-6).

2 (16:18) The religious leaders reject the Saviour, but He nevertheless will build His church. This word church, *ekklesia* in the Greek, often translated the word ''congregation'' in the Septuagint (the Greek Version of the Old Testament, 270 B.C.). Christ blesses Peter (''Rock'' in Greek; *Petros*) and declares that now He will build His congregation upon the rockshelf *(petra)* truth that He is the Christ, the Son of God.

3 (16:19) All the apostles receive this authority in Matthew 18:18. In the Book of Acts and in the Epistles they used this authority to establish the Church as the Spirit led them.

Conditions of Discipleship

24 Then said Jesus unto His disciples, If any *man* will come after Me, let him deny himself, and take up his cross, and follow Me.
25 For whosoever will save his life shall lose it; and whosoever will lose his life for My sake shall find it.
26 For what is a man profited, if he shall gain the whole world, and lose his own soul? Or what shall a man give in exchange for his soul?

Kingdom Promised
Mark 8:39-9:1
Luke 9:26-27

27 For the Son of man shall come in the glory of His Father with His angels, and then He shall reward every man according to his works.
1 28 Verily I say unto you, There are some standing here, who shall not taste of death, till they see the Son of man coming in His kingdom.

CHAPTER 17
The Transfiguration
A Look into the Future Kingdom
● *Mountain (Tabor or Hermon)*
Mark 9:2-13
Luke 9:28-36

1 And after six days Jesus taketh Peter, James, and John, his brother, and bringeth them up into an high mountain privately,
2 And was transfigured before them; and His face did shine like the sun, and His raiment was *as* white as the light.

3 And, behold, there appeared unto them Moses and Elijah talking with Him.
4 Then answered Peter, and said unto Jesus, Lord, it is good for us to be here; if thou wilt, let us make here three booths; one for thee, and one for Moses, and one for Elijah.
5 While he yet spoke, behold, a 2 bright cloud overshadowed them; and, behold, a voice out of the cloud, which said, This is My beloved Son, in whom I am well pleased; hear ye Him.
6 And when the disciples heard *it,* they fell on their face, and were very much afraid.
7 And Jesus came and touched them, and said, Arise, and be not afraid.
8 And when they had lifted up their eyes, they saw no man, except Jesus only.
9 And as they came down from the mountain, Jesus charged them, saying, Tell the vision to no man, until the Son of man is raised again from the dead.
10 And His disciples asked Him, 3 saying, Why then say the scribes that Elijah must first come?
11 And Jesus answered and said unto them, Elijah truly shall first come, and restore all things.
12 But I say unto you, That Elijah is 4 come already, and they knew him not, but have done unto him whatsoever they desired. Likewise shall also the Son of man suffer of them.

---

1 (16:28) The Transfiguration, Matthew 17:2, was a foreglimpse of Christ's future Kingdom glory.

2 (17:5) See 2 Peter 1:15-28 for Peter's later testimony on this event.

3 (17:10) Behold, I will send you Elijah the prophet before the coming of the great and dreadful day of the Lord:

And he shall turn the heart of the fathers to the children, and the heart of the children to their fathers, lest I come and smite the earth with a curse (Malachi 4:5-6).

4 (17:12) Malachi 3:1 foretells the coming of John the Baptist.

PAST	PRESENT	RAPTURE	FIRST 3½ LAST 3½ TRIBULATION		ARMA-GEDDON	MIL-LENNIUM	NEW HEAVENS & EARTH

(Matthew 16:18)

THE STONE and the ROCK

In St. Peter's Cathedral in the Vatican is a statue of Peter seated on a chair. His feet are bare. The toes on one foot have been worn smooth by the multiplied thousands of people who have passed by and kissed this statue.

This misdirected allegiance is caused in part because people are not aware of the true meaning of verse 18. The verse is a play on words to convey the omnipotence (almighty power) of God.

"Thou are Peter (**petros, a rock**), and upon this rock (**petra, a massive rock**) I will build My church."

The church is built on Christ Himself...and not on the stone of Peter. Read 1 Peter 2:4-8 and 1 Corinthians 3:11.

Peter was a wonderful Christian in many ways. Here in Matthew 16:16 he stood like a **rock** (this was the meaning of his name, John 1:42). Yet at other times he showed that only Christ, not he himself, was the infallible rock upon which the church was to be built (Matthew 16:22-23; Luke 22:55-62; Galatians 2:11,14).

Thousands daily kiss Peter's feet in St. Peter's Cathedral in the Vatican.

13 Then the disciples understood that He spoke unto them of John the Baptist.

**Christ's Power Demonstrated
To Powerless Disciples**
Mark 9:14-21
Luke 9:37-43

14 And when they were come to the multitude, there came to Him a *certain* man, kneeling down to Him, and saying,
15 Lord, have mercy on my son; for he is epileptic, and greatly vexed; for often he falleth into the fire, and often into the water.
16 And I brought him to thy disciples, and they could not cure him.
17 Then Jesus answered and said, O faithless and perverse generation, how long shall I be with you? How long shall I bear with you? Bring him here to Me.
18 And Jesus rebuked the demon, and he departed out of him; and the child was cured from that very hour.
19 Then came the disciples to Jesus privately, and said, Why could not we cast him out?
20 And Jesus said unto them, Because of your unbelief; for verily I say unto you, If ye have faith as a grain of mustard seed, ye shall say unto this mountain, Move from here to yonder place; and it shall move; and nothing shall be impossible unto you.
21 Howbeit, this kind goeth not out except by prayer and fasting.

**Jesus Again Foretells
His Death and Resurrection**
● *Galilee*
Mark 9:30-32
Luke 9:43-45

22 And while they abode in Galilee, Jesus said unto them, The Son of man shall be betrayed into the hands of men,
23 And they shall kill Him, and the third day He shall be raised again. And they were exceedingly sorry.

**The Miracle of the
Tribute Money**
● *Capernaum*

24 And when they were come to Capernaum, they that received tribute *money* came to Peter, and said, Doth not your master pay tribute?
25 He saith, Yes, And when he was come into the house, Jesus spoke first to him saying, What thinkest thou, Simon? Of whom do the kings of the earth take custom or tribute? Of their own sons, or of strangers?
26 Peter saith unto Him, Of strangers. Jesus saith unto him, Then are the sons free.
27 Notwithstanding, lest we should offend them, go thou to the sea, and cast an hook, and take up the fish that first cometh up. And when thou hast opened its mouth, thou shalt find a piece of money; that take, and give unto them for Me and thee.

CHAPTER 18

Ambition of Disciples Rebuked
● *Capernaum*
Matthew 8:19-22
Mark 9:33-50
Luke 9:46-62

1 At the same time came the disciples unto Jesus, saying, Who is the greatest in the kingdom of heaven?
2 And Jesus called a little child unto Him, and set him in the midst of them,
3 And said, Verily I say unto you, Except ye be converted, and become as little children, ye shall not enter into the kingdom of heaven.
4 Whosoever, therefore, shall humble himself as this little child, the same is greatest in the kingdom of heaven.
5 And whosoever shall receive one such little child in My name receiveth Me.

PAST	PRESENT	RAPTURE	FIRST 3½ LAST 3½ TRIBULATION	ARMA-GEDDON	MIL-LENNIUM	NEW HEAVENS & EARTH

Vietnamese children outside hospital in Nha Trang.

(Matthew 18:4,5)

THE FAITH OF A CHILD

I took this photograph in Vietnam. Around me were the sounds of war...the helicopters, the sounds of falling bombs, the cries of the sick and the dying. Outside a hospital I saw these children, who in spite of many adversities, eagerly looked into my camera, full of happy smiles. What a contrast!

Childlike faith dispels all doubts and glooms...is not concerned with personal gain. The disciples in Matthew 18:1 were bickering for position...and Christ wisely used the illustration of the humility and faith of the little child to convey a most important lesson to each of us.

1 6 But whosoever shall offend one of these little ones who believe in Me, it were better for him that a millstone were hanged about his neck, and *that* he were drowned in the depth of the sea.

Stumbling Blocks

7 Woe unto the world because of offenses! For it must needs be that offenses come; but woe to that man by whom the offense cometh!

8 Wherefore, if thy hand or thy foot offend thee, cut it off, and cast *it* from thee; it is better for thee to enter into life lame or maimed, rather than, having two hands or two feet, to be cast into everlasting fire.

9 And if thine eye offend thee, pluck it out, and cast *it* from thee; it is better for thee to enter into life with one eye, rather than, having two eyes, to be cast into hell fire.

10 Take heed that ye despise not one of these little ones; for I say unto you that in heaven their angels do always behold the face of My Father, who is in heaven.

11 For the Son of man is come to save that which was lost.

12 How think ye? If a man have an hundred sheep, and one of them be gone astray, doth he not leave the ninety and nine, and goeth into the mountains, and seeketh that which is gone astray?

13 And if so be that he find it, verily I say unto you, he rejoiceth more over that *sheep* than over the ninety and nine which went not astray.

14 Even so it is not the will of your Father, who is in heaven, that one of these little ones should perish.

Steps for Discipline and Forgiveness

15 Moreover, if thy brother shall trespass against thee, go and tell him his fault between thee and him alone; if he shall hear thee, thou hast gained thy brother.

16 But if he will not hear *thee, then* take with thee one or two more, that in the mouth of two or three witnesses every word may be established.

17 And if he shall neglect to hear them, tell *it* unto the church; but if he neglect to hear the church, let him be unto thee as an heathen man and a tax collector.

18 Verily I say unto you, Whatsoever ye shall bind on earth shall be bound in heaven; and whatsoever ye shall loose on earth shall be loosed in heaven. 2

19 Again I say unto you that if two of you shall agree on earth as touching any thing that they shall ask, it shall be done for them by My Father, who is in heaven.

20 For where two or three are gathered together in My name, there am I in the midst of them.

21 Then came Peter to Him, and said, Lord, how often shall my brother sin against me, and I forgive him? Till seven times?

22 Jesus saith unto him, I say not unto thee, Until seven times; but, Until seventy times seven.

23 Therefore is the kingdom of heaven likened unto a certain king, who would take account of his servants.

24 And when he had begun to reckon, one was brought unto him, who owed him ten thousand talents.

25 But forasmuch as he had nothing *with which* to pay, his lord commanded him to be sold, and his wife, and children, and all that he had, and payment to be made.

26 The servant, therefore, fell down, and worshiped him, saying, Lord, have patience with me, and I will pay thee all.

27 Then the lord of that servant was moved with compassion, and loosed him, and forgave him the debt.

28 But the same servant went out, and found one of his fellow ser-

vants, who owed him an hundred denarii; and he laid hands on him and took *him* by the throat, saying, Pay me what thou owest.

29 And his fellow servant fell down at his feet, and besought him, saying, Have patience with me, and I will pay thee all.

30 And he would not, but went and cast him into prison, till he should pay the debt.

31 So when his fellow servants saw what was done, they were very sorry, and came and told unto their lord all that was done.

32 Then his lord, after he had called him, said unto him, O thou wicked servant, I forgave thee all that debt, because thou besoughtest me!

33 Shouldest not thou also have had compassion on thy fellow servant, even as I had pity on thee?

34 And his lord was angry, and delivered him to the inquisitors, till he should pay all that was due unto him.

1 35 So likewise shall My heavenly Father do also unto you, if ye, from your hearts, forgive not every one his brother his trespasses.

CHAPTER 19

Concerning Divorce
c. September 29 A.D.
Mark 10:2-12

1 And it came to pass *that,* when Jesus had finished these sayings, He departed from Galilee, and came into the borders of Judaea beyond *the* Jordan.

2 And great multitudes followed Him, and He healed them there.

3 The Pharisees also came unto Him, testing Him, and saying unto Him, Is it lawful for a man to put away his wife for every cause?

4 And He answered and said unto them, Have ye not read that He who

made *them* at the beginning, made them male and female;

5 And said, For this cause shall a man leave father and mother, and shall cleave to his wife, and they two shall be one flesh?

6 Wherefore, they are no more two, but one flesh. What, therefore, God hath joined together, let not man put asunder.

7 They say unto Him, Why did Moses then command to give a writing of divorcement, and to put her away?

8 He saith unto them, Moses, because of the hardness of your hearts, permitted you to put away your wives, but from the beginning it was not so.

9 And I say unto you, Whosoever shall put away his wife, except *it be* for fornication, and shall marry another, committeth adultery; and whosoever marrieth her who is put away doth commit adultery.

10 His disciples say unto Him, If the case of the man be so with *his* wife, it is not good to marry.

11 But He said unto them, All *men* cannot receive this saying, except *they* to whom it is given.

12 For there are some eunuchs, who were so born from *their* mother's womb; and there are some eunuchs, who were made eunuchs by men; and there are eunuchs, who have made themselves eunuchs for the kingdom of heaven's sake. He that is able to receive *it,* let him receive *it.*

Jesus Blesses Children
• *Perea*
Mark 10:13-16
Luke 18:15-17

13 Then were there brought unto Him little children, that He should put *His* hands on them, and pray; and the disciples rebuked them.

1 (18:35) All men have a duty to forgive. Believers at the Judgment seat of Christ (II Corinthians 5:10) and unbelievers at the Final Judgment (Revelation 20:11-15) will be held responsible for this.

PAST	PRESENT	RAPTURE	FIRST 3½ LAST 3½ TRIBULATION		ARMA-GEDDON	MIL-LENNIUM	NEW HEAVENS & EARTH

(Matthew 18:20)

THE GROUPS CHRIST HONORS

On May 3, 1971 many young people became again concerned about the war in Vietnam. The converging on Washington, D.C. was for one basic purpose, that of disrupting the Government. In the long hours through the night many resorted to drugs. They gathered in groups of 2 and 3 and in groups of many hundreds and thousands. But their purposes were not God-centered. Their actions were not Christ-inspired. And in seeking for peace, they resorted to violence. 7000 were arrested.

What a contrast to the verses of promise in 19 and 20. For when just 2 or 3 gather in Christ's name, seeking to do His will...then, and only then, is Christ in the midst of such a gathering. It is not the multitude that is important; but rather that which counts is the faith and the sincere devotion of those who meet.

Youth with Viet Cong flag atop statue in Washington, D.C.

(Matthew 19:5)

THE NO-MARRIAGE MARRIAGES

In 1920 the percentage of divorces to marriages was 8%. The divorce rate is now over 13%. Over 4 million people in the U.S. are now divorced.

Many well-known motion picture personalities unashamedly make public the fact that they participate in "no-marriage" marriages. What this means is that they live together in a husband-wife relationship, have children, but actually do not get married. Then, at their convenience, they separate.

The Pill has helped in destroying the sanctity of marriage as well. The Biblical principles of marriage are being ignored even by many once-evangelical churches.

New Set of Morals, Family Shift Seen in Next 3 Decades

14 But Jesus said, Permit little children, and forbid them not, to come unto Me; for of such is the kingdom of heaven.

15 And He laid *His* hands on them, and departed from there.

The Rich Young Ruler
30 A.D.
● *Perea*
Mark 10:17-31
Luke 18:18-30

16 And, behold, one came and said unto Him, Good Master, what good thing shall I do, that I may have eternal life?

17 And He said unto him, Why callest thou Me good? *There is* none good but one, *that is*, God; but if thou wilt enter into life, keep the commandments.

18 He saith unto Him, Which? Jesus said, Thou shalt do no murder, Thou shalt not commit adultery, Thou shalt not steal, Thou shalt not bear false witness,

19 Honor thy father and *thy* mother; and, Thou shalt love thy neighbor as thyself.

20 The young man saith unto Him, All these things have I kept from my youth up. What lack I yet?

21 Jesus said unto him, If thou wilt be perfect, go *and* sell what thou hast, and give to the poor, and thou shalt have treasure in heaven; and come *and* follow Me.

22 But when the young man heard that saying, he went away sorrowful; for he had great possessions.

23 Then said Jesus unto His disciples, Verily I say unto you that a rich man shall with difficulty enter into the kingdom of heaven.

24 And again I say unto you, It is easier for a camel to go through the eye of a needle, than for a rich man to enter into the kingdom of God.

25 When His disciples heard *it,* they were exceedingly amazed, saying, Who, then, can be saved?

26 But Jesus beheld *them,* and said unto them, With men this is impossible, but with God all things are possible.

Rewards of Discipleship

27 Then answered Peter and said unto Him, Behold, we have forsaken all, and followed thee. What shall we have, therefore?

28 And Jesus said unto them, Verily I say unto you that ye who have followed Me, in the regeneration, when the Son of man shall sit on the throne of His glory, ye also shall sit upon twelve thrones, judging the twelve tribes of Israel.

29 And every one that hath forsaken houses, or brethren, or sisters, or father, or mother, or wife, or children, or lands, for My name's sake, shall receive an hundredfold, and shall inherit everlasting life.

30 But many *that are* first shall be last, and the last *shall be* first.

CHAPTER 20

**Parable of the Laborers
in the Vineyard**

1 For the kingdom of heaven is like a man *that is* an householder, who went out early in the morning to hire laborers into his vineyard.

2 And when he had agreed with the laborers for a denarius a day, he sent them into his vineyard.

3 And he went out about the third hour, and saw others standing idle in the market place.

4 And said unto them, Go ye also into the vineyard, and whatever is right, I will give you. And they went their way.

5 Again he went out about the sixth and ninth hour, and did the same.

6 And about the eleventh hour he went out, and found others standing idle, and saith unto them, Why stand ye here all the day idle?

7 They say unto him, Because no man hath hired us. He saith unto them, Go ye also into the vineyard, and whatever is right, *that* shall ye receive.

8 So when evening was come, the lord of the vineyard saith unto his steward, Call the laborers, and give

Advertising Notes

Seagram's Christmas Ads Will Cost $6 Million

The various divisions of Joseph E. Seagram & Sons, Inc., will ring in the ... mas season ...

The Leisure Class

Firms, Workers Cheer As the Four-Day Week Makes Some Inroads

Productivity, Morale Raised; Absenteeism, Quitting Cut; But a Union Leader Demurs

More Time for Picking Apples

By WILLIAM M. CARLEY AND TIM METZ
Staff Reporters of THE WALL STREET JOURNAL
... ank God it's Thursday.
what L. C. Clayton of Braintree,

material.

The Calvert Distillers ... pany division will spend 600,000 on advertising 575,000 on sales pro... red to the Christmas ... he Four Roses D ... any division ha... million for hob... g and sales pr... vs by the oth... ram sales d... rt Distillers ... Wine & Sp... Park ... will lift t... well pas...

Drugs on the Job

Heroin, Marijuana Use By Workers, Applicants Climbs at Some Firms

New York Telephone Finds A Dope Ring; Brokers Consult Former Addicts

Smoking Pot in the Office

By ALFRED L. MALABRE JR.
Staff Reporter of THE WALL STREET JOURNAL
NEW YORK—Corporations are getting their first close-up look at the drug problem.
The company's alcoholic has been ...
sells ...

... resents a strong schedule ... newspaper and ... Sea-

(Matthew 19:24)

THE RICH YOUNG RULER'S MISTAKES

The rich young ruler made mistakes that many who are seeking make even today.

(1) The rich man thought of Christ as a good teacher. And many today follow cults which include Christ in their assembly of leaders...recognizing Him simply as a great teacher of His day. But Christ answers this in verse 17 by showing that it is inadequate to affirm Him to be merely **good**, without acknowledging Him to be the God-man Messiah sent from the Father.

(2) The rich young ruler thought the way to heaven (salvation) could be attained by good works. Many today mistakenly believe that their good works will gain them entrance into heaven. Isaiah 64:6 tells us that "...all our righteousnesses are as filthy rags...."

(3) The most tragic mistake of the rich young ruler was in not following the final words of Christ. They were "...come and follow Me" (verse 21).

Is it no wonder that Christ said, "...it is easier for a camel to go through the eye of a needle..."

Man, surrounded by his riches and good works, finds it extremely difficult to abandon all and by faith alone, to accept Christ. And it thus stands to reason that as those in the United States become more affluent, they will become more godless. We can already see this happening today.

them *their* hire, beginning from the last unto the first.

9 And when they came that *were hired* about the eleventh hour, they received every man a denarius.

10 But when the first came, they supposed that they should have received more; and they likewise received every man a denarius.

11 And when they had received *it,* they murmured against the house-holder,

12 Saying, These last have worked *but* one hour, and thou hast made them equal unto us, who have borne the burden and heat of the day.

13 But he answered one of them, and said, Friend, I do thee no wrong. Didst not thou agree with me for a denarius?

14 Take *what is* thine, and go thy way; I will give unto this last, even as unto thee.

15 Is it not lawful for me to do what I will with mine own? Is thine eye evil, because I am good?

1 16 So the last shall be first, and the first last; for many are called, but few chosen.

Jesus Predicts Death and Resurrection
● *Near Jordan*
Mark 10:32-34
Luke 18:31-34

17 And Jesus, going up to Jerusalem, took the twelve disciples aside along the way, and said unto them,

18 Behold, we go up to Jerusalem; and the Son of man shall be be-trayed unto the chief priests and unto·the scribes, and they shall con-demn Him to death,

19 And shall deliver Him to the Gen-tiles to mock, and to scourge, and to crucify *Him.* And the third day He shall rise again.

A Mother's Ambition for Sons James and John
Mark 10:35-45

20 Then came to Him the mother of Zebedee's children with her sons, worshiping *Him,* and desiring a cer-tain thing of Him.

21 And He said unto her, What wilt thou? She saith unto Him, Grant that these, my two sons, may sit, the one on thy right hand, and the other on the left, in thy kingdom.

22 But Jesus answered and said, Ye know not what ye ask. Are ye able to drink of the cup that I shall drink of, and to be baptized with the bap-tism that I am baptized with? They say unto Him, We are able.

23 And He saith unto them, Ye shall drink indeed of My cup, and be bap-tized with the baptism that I am baptized with, but to sit on My right hand, and on My left, is not Mine to give, but *it shall be given to them* for whom it is prepared by My Fa-ther.

24 And when the ten heard *it,* they were moved with indignation against the two brethren.

25 But Jesus called them *unto Him,* and said, Ye know that the princes of the Gentiles exercise dominion over them, and they that are great exercise authority over them.

26 But it shall not be so among you, but whosoever will be great among you, let him be your minister.

27 And whosoever will be chief among you, let him be your servant;

28 Even as the Son of man came not to be ministered unto, but to minister, and to give His life a ransom for many.

Two Blind Men Healed
● *Jericho*
Mark 10:46-52
Luke 18:35-43

29 And as they departed from Jericho, a great multitude followed Him.

1 (20:16) This reversal of positions will take place at Christ's Second Coming at the judgments fol-lowing both the Rapture and Armageddon.

PAST	PRESENT	RAPTURE	FIRST 3½	LAST 3½ TRIBULATION	ARMA-GEDDON	MIL-LENNIUM	NEW HEAVENS & EARTH

In your prayer life, rest by the sea of Galilee and take inventory of the direction in which you are going. Are you living a life of wood, hay and stubble or one that will garner Crowns at the Judgment seat of Christ?

(Matthew 20:3)

THE BUSY IDLE CHRISTIANS

Is it possible to be busy and yet idle? At first glance these may appear to be direct opposites.

It isn't enough just to be busy. What are you busy about? Have you glanced around your church lately? at its activities? Is it a beehive of activity? Are you running back in forth to church engaged in this or that without a moment to yourself? If this is a picture of your daily life...it is quite possible you could be an idle Christian.

Many Christians are busy in "church work" but are really idle in the main callings of the "work of the church." There is a difference. Get into the vineyard alone with God, spend time alone with the Lord and He will direct your energies so that souls will be saved and saints uplifted, and so that you may glorify Him in all that you do (Acts 6:2-4).

30 And, behold, two blind men sitting by the wayside, when they heard that Jesus passed by, cried out, saying, Have mercy on us, O Lord, *thou* Son of David.

31 And the multitude rebuked them, that they should hold their peace; but they cried the more, saying, Have mercy on us, O Lord, *thou* Son of David.

32 And Jesus stood still, and called them, and said, What will ye that I shall do unto you?

33 They say unto Him, Lord, that our eyes may be opened.

34 So Jesus had compassion *on them,* and touched their eyes; and immediately their eyes received sight, and they followed Him.

CHAPTER 21

**Christ's Last Week —
The Triumphal Entry**
Sunday, April, 30 A.D.
● *Jerusalem*
**Jesus' Denunciation
of Scribes and Pharisees**

1 And when they drew near unto Jerusalem, and were come to Bethphage, unto the Mount of Olives, then sent Jesus two disciples,

2 Saying unto them, Go into the village opposite you, and straightway ye shall find an ass tied, and a colt with her; loose *them,* and bring *them* unto Me.

3 And if any *man* say anything unto you, ye shall say, The Lord hath need of them; and straightway he will send them.

1 4 All this was done, that it might be fulfilled which was spoken by the prophet, saying,

5 Tell ye the daughter of Zion, Behold, thy King cometh unto thee, meek, and sitting upon an ass, and a colt, the foal of an ass.

6 And the disciples went, and did as Jesus commanded them,

7 And brought the ass, and the colt, and put on them their clothes, and they set *Him* thereon.

8 And a very great multitude spread their garments in the way; others cut down branches from the trees, and spread *them* in the way.

9 And the multitudes that went 2 before, and that followed, cried, saying, Hosanna to the Son of David! Blessed *is* He that cometh in the name of the Lord! Hosanna in the highest!

**Jesus Drives Traders and
Moneychangers from Temple**
● *Jerusalem*
Mark 11:12-18
Luke 19:45-48

10 And when He was come into Jerusalem, all the city was moved, saying, Who is this?

11 And the multitude said, This is Jesus, the prophet of Nazareth of Galilee.

Monday, April, 30 A.D.

12 And Jesus went into the temple of God, and cast out all them that sold and bought in the temple, and overthrew the tables of the moneychangers, and the seats of them that sold doves,

13 And said unto them, It is written, 3 My house shall be called the house of prayer, but ye have made it a den of thieves.

14 And the blind and the lame came to Him in the temple, and He healed them.

1 (21:4) Rejoice greatly, O daughter of Zion; shout, O daughter of Jerusalem: behold, thy King cometh unto thee: He is just, and having salvation; lowly, and riding upon an ass, and upon a colt the foal of an ass (Zechariah 9:9).

2 (21:9) Blessed be He that cometh in the name of the Lord: we have blessed you out of the house of the Lord (Psalm 118:26).

3 (21:13) Even them will I bring to My holy mountain, and make them joyful in My house of prayer: their burnt-offerings and their sacrifices shall be accepted upon Mine altar; for Mine house shall be called an house of prayer for all people (Isaiah 56:7).

15 And when the chief priests and scribes saw the wonderful things that He did, and the children crying in the temple, and saying, Hosanna to the Son of David! they were very displeased,

16 And said unto Him, Hearest thou what these say? And Jesus saith unto them, Yea; have ye never read, Out of the mouth of babes and sucklings thou hast perfected praise?

17 And He left them, and went out of the city into Bethany; and He lodged there.

The Fig Tree with No Fruit
● *Bethany to Jerusalem*
Mark 11:19-26

18 Now in the morning, as He returned into the city, He was hungry.

19 And when He saw a fig tree along the way, He came to it, and found nothing on it but leaves only, and said unto it, Let no fruit grow on thee henceforward forever. And presently the fig tree withered away.

20 And when the disciples saw *it*, they marveled, saying, How soon is the fig tree withered away!

21 Jesus answered and said unto them, Verily I say unto you, If ye have faith, and doubt not, ye shall not only do this *which is done* to the fig tree, but also, if ye shall say unto this mountain, Be thou removed, and be thou cast into the sea, it shall be done.

22 And all things, whatever ye shall ask in prayer, believing, ye shall receive.

Authority of Jesus Questioned
● *Jerusalem*

23 And when He was come into the temple, the chief priests and the elders of the people came unto Him as He was teaching, and said, By what authority doest thou these things? And who gave thee this authority?

24 And Jesus answered and said unto them, I also will ask you one thing, which, if ye tell me, I likewise, will tell you by what authority I do these things.

25 The baptism of John, from where was it? From heaven, or of men? And they reasoned with themselves, saying, If we shall say, From heaven; He will say unto us, Why did ye not then believe him?

26 But if we shall say, From men: we fear the people; for all hold John as a prophet.

27 And they answered Jesus, and said, We cannot tell. And He said unto them, Neither tell I you by what authority I do these things.

Parable of Two Sons

28 But what think ye? A *certain* man had two sons; and he came to the first, and said, Son, go work today in my vineyard.

29 He answered and said, I will not; but afterward he repented, and went.

30 And he came to the second, and said the same. And he answered and said I *go*, sir; and went not.

31 Which of the two did the will of *his* father? They say unto Him, The first. Jesus saith unto them, Verily I say unto you that the tax collectors and the harlots go into the kingdom of God before you.

32 For John came unto you in the way of righteousness, and ye believed him not; but the tax collectors and the harlots believed him; and ye, when ye had seen *it*, repented not afterward, that ye might believe him.

Parable of the Wicked Landowner
Mark 12:1-9
Luke 20:9-19

33 Hear another parable: There was a certain householder, who planted a vineyard, and hedged it round about, and dug a winepress in it, and built a tower, and leased it to *tenant* farmers, and went into a far country.

PAST	PRESENT	RAPTURE	FIRST 3½ LAST 3½ TRIBULATION		ARMA-GEDDON	MIL-LENNIUM	NEW HEAVENS & EARTH

Photograph taken on the Mount of Olives dramatically portrays Matthew 21:2. This is a familiar scene even in present-day Jerusalem.

Panoramic view of Inner City wall of Jerusalem. In the center of photograph is the Golden Gate, sometimes called the Eastern Gate. This is the only gate that leads directly into the temple area.

(Matthew 21:10)

GOLDEN GATE, DIRECT ENTRANCE TO TEMPLE AREA

When Jesus entered Jerusalem it was probably through a gate located approximately where the Golden Gate, now walled up, stands. The Golden Gate is on the east side of the city facing the Mount of Olives. The gate was closed by the Turkish governor of Jerusalem in 1530 A.D. in the hope of postponing the day of judgment and the end of the world. Many Christians believe that when Jesus comes again, the gate will be opened and He will once again enter the Holy City (Ezekiel 44:1-3). If the gate were open it would be the only gate that would lead directly to the temple area.

Bethany is located 1-3/4 miles from Jerusalem on the eastern slope of the Mount of Olives. It is on the road to Jericho. Here was the home of Mary, Martha and Lazarus (John 11:1).

A fig tree at Jerusalem, in full leaf, before invasion of locusts.

The same tree 15 minutes later, completely denuded of every leaf by a locust swarm.

(Matthew 21:19)

THE LESSON OF THE FIG TREE

The lesson of the withered fig tree may well be applied to Israel and also to the fruitlessness of any people at any time. Christ looked to Israel for fruit, and He only found leaves of show—for He was rejected.

Does the Christendom of the United States contain fruit, or leaves only? Observe the churches in your own community.

Popular theologians of the day may capture the limelight of the newspapers but if their message is not grounded in the Word of God... their ministry will wither as the fig tree.

And, as to the fig tree, judgment will come swift and sure (verse 19-20).

34 And when the time of the fruit drew near, he sent his servants to the farmers, that they might receive the fruits of it.

35 And the farmers took his servants, and beat one, and killed another, and stoned another.

36 Again, he sent other servants more than the first; and they did the same unto them.

37 But last of all he sent unto them his son, saying, They will reverence my son.

1 38 But when the farmers saw the son, they said among themselves, This is the heir; come, let us kill him, and let us seize on his inheritance.

39 And they caught him, and cast *him* out of the vineyard, and slew *him*.

40 When the lord, therefore, of the vineyard cometh, what will he do unto those farmers?

41 They say unto him, He will miserably destroy those wicked men, and will lease *his* vineyard unto other farmers, who shall render him the fruits in their seasons.

42 Jesus saith unto them, Did ye never read in the scriptures, The stone which the builders rejected, the same is become the head of the corner; this is the Lord's doing, and it is marvelous in our eyes?

43 Therefore say I unto you, The kingdom of God shall be taken from you, and given to a nation bringing forth the fruits of it.

44 And whosoever shall fall on this stone shall be broken, but on whomsoever it shall fall, it will grind him to powder.

45 And when the chief priests and Pharisees had heard His parables, they perceived that He spoke of them.

46 But when they sought to lay hands on Him, they feared the multitude, because they regarded Him as a prophet.

CHAPTER 22

**Parable of the Marriage Feast
For the King's Son**
Luke 14:16-24

1 And Jesus answered and spoke   2
unto them again by parables, and said,

2 The kingdom of heaven is like a certain king, who made a marriage for his son,

3 And sent forth his servants to call them that were bidden to the wedding; and they would not come.

4 Again, he sent forth other servants, saying, Tell them who are bidden, Behold, I have prepared my dinner; my oxen and *my* fatlings *are* killed, and all things *are* ready; come unto the marriage.

5 But they made light of *it,* and went their ways, one to his farm, another to his merchandise;

6 And the remnant took his servants, and treated *them* shamefully, and slew *them.*

7 But when the king heard *of it,* he was angry; and he sent forth his armies, and destroyed those murderers, and burned up their city.

8 Then saith he to his servants, The wedding is ready, but they who were bidden were not worthy.

9 Go, therefore, into the highways, and as many as ye shall find, bid to the marriage.

1   (21:38-44) From verse 38 on, this parable prophetically foresees the rejection of Christ by the leaders of Israel, and the subsequent turning to Him of many Gentiles as prophesied in Isaiah 49:6.

2   (22:1-14) Behold the prophetic elements in this parable. Verse 3, Israel rejects her prophets; 4-6, the Apostles rejected; 7, Jerusalem destroyed and burned in A. D. 70; 8-10, the present day Gospel call; 11-14, the garment of Christ's righteousness alone can save the sinner from the Final Judgment.

PAST	PRESENT	RAPTURE	FIRST 3½	LAST 3½	ARMA-GEDDON	MIL-LENNIUM	NEW HEAVENS & EARTH
			TRIBULATION				

A close-up view of 2500 year old stones in walls at Jerusalem.

(Matthew 21:44)

STONES WITH A MESSAGE

To the Jew, Christ was a Stumbling Stone (Romans 9:32-33).

To the Church, Christ is the Foundation Stone (Ephesians 2:20-22).

To the Gentile world powers,

Christ will be the Smiting Stone (Daniel 2:34).

10 So those servants went out into the highways, and gathered together all, as many as they found, both bad and good; and the wedding was furnished with guests.

11 And when the king came in to see the guests, he saw there a man who had not on a wedding garment.

12 And he saith unto him, Friend, how camest thou in here not having a wedding garment? And he was speechless.

13 Then said the king to the servants, Bind him hand and foot, and take him away, and cast *him* into outer darkness; there shall be weeping and gnashing of teeth.

14 For many are called, but few *are* chosen.

**Tribute to Caesar
and Lawfulness of Taxes**
Tuesday, April 30 A.D.
● *Jerusalem*
Mark 12:13-17
Luke 20:20-26

15 Then went the Pharisees, and took counsel how they might entangle Him in *His* talk.

16 And they sent out unto Him their disciples with the Herodians, saying, Master, we know that thou art true, and teachest the way of God in truth, neither carest thou for any *man;* for thou regardest not the person of men.

17 Tell us, therefore, What thinkest thou? Is it lawful to give tribute unto Caesar, or not?

18 But Jesus perceived their wickedness, and said, Why test Me, *ye* hypocrites?

19 Show Me the tribute money. And they brought unto Him a denarius.

20 And He saith unto them, Whose *is* this image and superscription?

21 They say unto Him, Caesar's. Then saith He unto them, Render, therefore, unto Caesar the things which are Caesar's; and unto God, the things that are God's.

22 When they had heard *these words,* they marveled, and left Him, and went their way.

**Sadducees Question
the Resurrection**
● *Jerusalem*
Mark 12:18-27
Luke 20:27-40

23 The same day came to Him the Sadducees, who say that there is no resurrection, and asked Him,

24 Saying, Master, Moses said, If a man die, having no children, his brother shall marry his wife, and raise up seed unto his brother.

25 Now there were with us seven brethren; and the first, when he had married a wife, died and, having no issue, left his wife unto his brother;

26 Likewise the second also, and the third, unto the seventh.

27 And last of all the woman died also.

28 Therefore, in the resurrection whose wife shall she be of the seven? For they all had her.

29 Jesus answered and said unto them, Ye do err, not knowing the scriptures, nor the power of God.

30 For in the resurrection they neither marry, nor are given in marriage, but are like the angels of God in heaven.

31 But as touching the resurrection of the dead, have ye not read that which was spoken unto you by God, saying,

32 I am the God of Abraham, and the God of Isaac, and the God of Jacob? God is not the God of the dead, but of the living.

33 And when the multitude heard *this,* they were astonished at His doctrine.

**Pharisees Question
the Commandments**
● *Jerusalem*
Mark 12:28-34

34 But when the Pharisees had heard that He had put the Sadducees to silence, they were gathered together.

PAST	PRESENT	RAPTURE	FIRST 3½ LAST 3½ TRIBULATION		ARMA- GEDDON	MIL- LENNIUM	NEW HEAVENS & EARTH

(Matthew 22:14)

MANY CALLED; FEW CHOSEN

This difficult verse comes to us illuminated by its context, the 13 verse parable which precedes it. This parable portrays the invitation to come to God's salvation given through the ages to MANY. It also, however, shows historically and prophetically that in relative terms, only FEW actually are drawn to accept God's gracious invitation to forgiveness and eternal life. Thus MANY are **called** (invited to be saved—the universal call to all men is to come to Christ) but FEW are **chosen** (actually saved; effectively drawn to Christ by the Father through the working of the Holy Spirit. See John 6:44).

Caesar

(Matthew 22:19)

CAESAR OR CHRIST

As Greece stands in history for freedom, so Rome stands for order. Law was the most characteristic and lasting expression of the Roman spirit. The Roman constitution was based on a stream of precedents. The slave had no legal rights whatever. He was considered an "impersonal man." His children were all classed as illegitimate. If a slave ran away and was caught he could be branded or crucified. Augustus boasted that he had recaptured 30,000 runaway slaves and had crucified all who had not been claimed.

Slaves male or female might be immorally taken advantage of by their masters without legal redress.

The Denarius, sometimes erroneously referred to as a penny, was worth more than a hundred dimes in **buying power** in Jesus' day. Sunday School teachers and children have always wondered why any man would toil all day and receive only a penny. But the denarius, worth 18¢ in silver value was then worth about $10 in actual buying power in today's market.

The Herodians, knowing the swiftness and severity of Roman law and the value of money, hoped to trap Jesus but failed.

35 Then one of them, *who was* a lawyer, asked *Him a question,* testing Him, and saying,

36 Master, which *is* the great commandment in the law?

37 Jesus said unto him, Thou shalt love the Lord, thy God, with all thy heart, and with all thy soul, and with all thy mind.

38 This is the first and great commandment.

39 And the second *is* like it, Thou shalt love thy neighbor as thyself.

40 On these two commandments hang all the law and the prophets.

The Pharisees Silenced
●*Jerusalem*
Mark 12:35-37
Luke 20:41-44

41 While the Pharisees were gathered together, Jesus asked them,

1 42 Saying, What think ye of Christ? Whose son is He? They say unto Him, *The Son* of David.

43 He saith unto them, How, then, doth David, in *the* Spirit, call Him Lord, saying,

2 44 The Lord said unto my Lord, Sit thou on My right hand, till I make thine enemies thy footstool?

45 If David, then, call Him Lord, how is He his son?

46 And no man was able to answer Him a word, neither dared any *man* from that day forth ask Him any more *questions.*

CHAPTER 23

**Jesus'
Denunciation of
Scribes and Pharisees**
●*Jerusalem*
Mark 12:38-40
Luke 20:45-47

1 Then spoke Jesus to the multitude, and to His disciples,

2 Saying, The scribes and the Pharisees sit in Moses' seat.

3 All, therefore, whatever they bid you observe, *that* observe and do; but do not after their works; for they say, and do not.

4 For they bind heavy burdens and grievous to be borne, and lay *them* on men's shoulders, but they *themselves* will not move them with one of their fingers.

5 But all their works they do to be seen of men; they make broad their phylacteries, and enlarge the borders of their garments,

6 And love the uppermost places at feasts, and the chief seats in the synagogues,

7 And greetings in the market places, and to be called by men, Rabbi, Rabbi.

8 But be not ye called Rabbi; for one is your Master, *even* Christ, and all ye are brethren.

9 And call no *man* your father upon the earth; for one is your Father, who is in heaven.

10 Neither be ye called masters: for one is your Master, *even* Christ.

11 But he that is greatest among you shall be your servant.

3 12 And whosoever shall exalt himself shall be abased; and he that shall humble himself shall be exalted.

**Jesus Announces
Tribulations That Will Befall
The Pharisees**
Mark 12:38-40
Luke 20:47

13 But woe unto you, scribes and Pharisees, hypocrites! For ye shut up the kingdom of heaven against men; for ye neither go in *yourselves,* neither permit them that are entering to go in.

---

1 (22:42) Son of David is a Messianic title referring to the Christ, the final Son of David, Jeremiah 23:5-8; Isaiah 11:1,9 (Jesse was David's father).

2 (22:44) The Lord said unto my Lord, Sit thou at My right hand, until I make thine enemies thy footstool (Psalm 110:1).

3 (23:12) Now, and then at the Judgment.

PAST	PRESENT	RAPTURE	FIRST 3½ LAST 3½ TRIBULATION		ARMA-GEDDON	MIL-LENNIUM	NEW HEAVENS & EARTH

Young Jewish boy with prayer bands at Wailing Wall.

(Matthew 23:5)

OUTWARD APPEARANCES OF WORSHIP

Beginning around 2 B.C., all male Jews were expected to wear at morning prayers, except on sabbaths and festivals, two **phylacteries.** One was worn on their forehead (frontlet); the other on their left arm. This consisted of small leather cases containing 4 passages of Scripture from the Old Testament: Exodus 13:1-10; 13:11-16; Deuteronomy 6:4-9; 11:13-21.

Many also enlarged the commanded memorial fringes on their robes (Numbers 15:38-39). Outward adornments exist in Israel even today— for example some orthodox Jews wear elaborate fur hats at the Wailing Wall. Thus also many people throughout the world become involved in the trappings of religion, such as lighting candles, saying repetitive prayers, fingering beads...losing sight of the real message of Scripture.

14 Woe unto you, scribes and Pharisees, hypocrites! For ye devour widows' houses, and for a pretense make long prayers; therefore, ye shall receive the greater damnation.

15 Woe unto you, scribes and Pharisees, hypocrites! For ye compass sea and land to make one proselyte, and when he is made, ye make him twofold more the child of hell than yourselves.

16 Woe unto you, *ye* blind guides, who say, Whosoever shall swear by the temple, it is nothing; but whosoever shall swear by the gold of the temple, he is a debtor!

17 *Ye* fools and blind; for which is greater, the gold, or the temple that sanctifieth the gold?

18 And, Whosoever shall swear by the altar, it is nothing; but whosoever sweareth by the gift that is upon it, he is bound.

19 *Ye* fools and blind; for which *is* greater, the gift, or the altar that sanctifieth the gift?

20 Whosoever, therefore, shall swear by the altar, sweareth by it, and by all things on it.

21 And whosoever shall swear by the temple, sweareth by it, and by Him that dwelleth in it.

22 And he that shall swear by heaven, sweareth by the throne of God, and by Him who sitteth on it.

23 Woe unto you, scribes and Pharisees, hypocrites! For ye pay tithe of mint and anise and cummin, and have omitted the weightier *matters* of the law, justice, mercy, and faith; these ought ye to have done, and not to leave the other undone.

24 *Ye* blind guides, who strain at a gnat, and swallow a camel.

25 Woe unto you, scribes and Pharisees, hypocrites! For ye make clean the outside of the cup and of the platter, but within they are full of extortion and excess.

26 *Thou* blind Pharisee, cleanse first that *which is* within the cup and platter, that the outside of them may be clean also.

27 Woe unto you, scribes and Pharisees, hypocrites! For ye are like whited sepulchers, which indeed appear beautiful outward, but are within full of dead *men's* bones, and of all uncleanness.

28 Even so ye also outwardly appear righteous unto men, but within ye are full of hypocrisy and iniquity.

29 Woe unto you, scribes and Pharisees, hypocrites! Because ye build the tombs of the prophets, and garnish the sepulchers of the righteous,

30 And say, If we had been in the days of our fathers, we would not have been partakers with them in the blood of the prophets.

31 Wherefore, ye are witnesses against yourselves, that ye are the sons of them who killed the prophets.

32 Fill up, then, the measure of your fathers.

33 *Ye* serpents, *ye* generation of vipers, how can ye escape the damnation of hell?

34 Wherefore, behold, I send unto you prophets, and wise men, and scribes; and *some* of them ye shall kill and crucify, and *some* of them shall ye scourge in your synagogues, and persecute *them* from city to city,

35 That upon you may come all the righteous blood shed upon the earth, from the blood of righteous Abel unto the blood of Zechariah, son of Barachiah, whom ye slew between the temple and the altar.

36 Verily I say unto you, All these things shall come upon this generation. [1]

---

1 (23:36) Christ here speaks of the coming awful siege and destruction of Jerusalem, A. D. 69-70.

PAST	PRESENT	RAPTURE	FIRST 3½ LAST 3½ TRIBULATION	ARMA-GEDDON	MIL-LENNIUM	NEW HEAVENS & EARTH

"...Man looketh on the outward appearance, but the Lord looketh on the heart" (1 Samuel 16:7).

(Matthew 23:27)

THE BEAUTY THAT IS SKIN DEEP

It was the custom in March, after the heavy rains, to whitewash the graves. This was done to prevent priests from being defiled by contact with the dead. And these sepulchers or tombs had an outward beauty...but inside were unclean.

Someone once said, "A woman deserves no credit for her beauty at 16 but beauty at 60 is her own soul's doing." It is interesting to note that almost $2 Billion a year is spent by Americans in the purchase of cosmetics. Here are some other statistics on outward adornments:

Money spent annually in the U.S. on
Jewelry and watches	$3.5 Billion
Toiletries and hairpieces	$5 Billion

What a challenge to look into our own lives. If we are in Christ, our inner beauty should reflect in our outward walk.

Jesus Grieves Over Jerusalem
●*Jerusalem*
Luke 13:34-35

37 O Jerusalem, Jerusalem, *thou* that killest the prophets, and stonest them who are sent unto thee, how often would I have gathered thy children together, even as a hen gathereth her chickens under *her* wings, and ye would not!

38 Behold, your house is left unto you desolate.

1 39 For I say unto you, Ye shall not see Me henceforth, till ye shall say, Blessed *is* He that cometh in the name of the Lord.

CHAPTER 24

2 **Jesus Tells of The Future**
●*Mt. of Olives*
Mark 13:1-37
Luke 21:5-36

1 And Jesus went out, and departed from the temple; and His disciples came to *Him* to show Him the buildings of the temple.

3 2 And Jesus said unto them, See ye not all these things? Verily I say unto you, There shall not be left here one stone upon another, that shall not be thrown down.

When and What Signs

3 And as He sat upon the Mount of Olives, the disciples came unto Him privately, saying, Tell us, when shall these things be? And what *shall be* the sign of thy coming, and of the end of the age?

4 And Jesus answered and said unto them, Take heed that no man deceive you.

Daniel's 70th Week of Years
(See Daniel 9:27)
Mark 13:5-13

5 For many shall come in My name, 4
saying, I am Christ; and shall deceive many.

6 And ye shall hear of wars and rumors of wars; see that ye be not troubled; for all *these things* must come to pass, but the end is not yet.

7 For nation shall rise against nation, and kingdom against kingdom; and there shall be famines, and pestilences, and earthquakes, in various places.

8 All these *are* the beginning of sorrows.

9 Then shall they deliver you up to be afflicted, and shall kill you; and ye shall be hated of all nations for My name's sake.

10 And then shall many be offended, and shall betray one another, and shall hate one another.

11 And many false prophets shall rise, and shall deceive many.

12 And because iniquity shall abound, the love of many shall grow cold.

13 But he that shall endure unto the end, the same shall be saved.

14 And this gospel of the kingdom shall be preached in all the world for a witness unto all nations; and then shall the end come.

---

1 (23:39) In that day shall the Lord defend the inhabitants of Jerusalem; and he that is feeble among them at that day shall be as David; and the house of David shall be as God, as the angel of the Lord before them (Zechariah 12:8). Also see Zechariah 13:1.

2 (24-25) These two chapters comprise the Olivet Discourse.

3 (24:2) Destruction of Jerusalem by the Romans in A. D. 70.

4 (24:5-13) Here Christ describes events which began in the past, continue in the present, and which will greatly increase during the first half of the Tribulation period, "the beginning of sorrows" (Verse 8).

PAST	PRESENT	RAPTURE	FIRST 3½ LAST 3½ TRIBULATION		ARMA-GEDDON	MIL-LENNIUM	NEW HEAVENS & EARTH

Just 47 seconds after 6 A.M., February 9, 1971 an earthquake struck
California leaving over 60 dead and thousands injured. Upheavals
tossed chunks of Golden State Freeway around like children's blocks
killing two men whose truck was squashed; causing property damage
into the millions.

(Matthew 24:7)

CALIFORNIANS IGNORE EARTHQUAKE

On February 9, 1971 a sudden thrusting movement within the broad
network of the San Andreas fault cost 64 lives near Los Angeles. Yet,
in spite of this devastating earthquake...just 2-1/2 months later...busi-
ness went on as usual. Millions continue to ignore this warning and
the peril of a future cataclysmic quake. All along this 600-mile fracture
in the earth's crust, Californians are living as if there never will be
another.

Scriptures tell us differently. For more severe earthquakes are yet in
store for this earth. And these will be but the beginning of sorrows
(verse 8). We, however, who are trusting in Christ and looking for His
Second Coming have a hope that transcends any present fear of earthquakes which we might legitimately have.

The Middle of Daniel's 70th Week Known as the Abomination of Desolation
Mark 13:14-18

1   15 When ye, therefore, shall see the abomination of desolation, spoken of by Daniel the prophet, stand in the holy place (whosoever readeth, let him understand),

16 Then let them who are in Judaea flee into the mountains;

17 Let him who is on the housetop not come down to take anything out of his house;

18 Neither let him who is in the field return back to take his clothes.

19 And woe unto those who are with child, and to those who nurse *children* in those days!

2   20 But pray that your flight be not in the winter, neither on the sabbath day;

The Great Tribulation (The Latter 3½ Years of the Week)
Mark 13:19-23
Luke 21:23-24

21 For then shall be great tribulation, such as was not since the beginning of the world to this time, no, nor ever shall be.

22 And except those days should be shortened, there should no flesh be saved; but for the elect's sake those days shall be shortened.

23 Then if any man shall say unto you, Lo, here *is* Christ, or there; believe *it* not.

24 For there shall arise false Christs, and false prophets, and shall show great signs and wonders, insomuch that, if *it were* possible, they shall deceive the very elect.

25 Behold, I have told you before.

26 Wherefore, if they shall say unto you, Behold, He is in the desert; go not forth: behold *He* is in the secret chambers; believe *it* not.

27 For as the lightning cometh out of the east, and shineth even unto the west, so shall also the coming of the Son of man be.

28 For wherever the carcass is, there will the eagles be gathered together.

Close of Tribulation The King Returns to Earth
Mark 13:24-27
Luke 21:29-33

29 Immediately after the tribulation of those days shall the sun be darkened, and the moon shall not give its light, and the stars shall fall from heaven, and the powers of the heavens shall be shaken.

30 And then shall appear the sign 3 of the Son of man in heaven; and then shall all the tribes of the earth mourn, and they shall see the Son of man coming in the clouds of heaven with power and great glory.

31 And He shall send His angels with a great sound of a trumpet, and they shall gather together His elect from the four winds, from one end of heaven to the other.

---

1   (24:15) This begins the final 3½ years of the 7 year Tribulation Period.

And he shall confirm the covenant with many for one week: and in the midst of the week he shall cause the sacrifice and the oblation to cease, and for the overspreading of abominations he shall make it desolate, even until the consummation, and that determined shall be poured upon the desolate (Daniel 9:27). Titus in A.D. 70 never fulfilled this. The plight of Jerusalem in the Roman siege of A.D. 69-70 was only a type of these coming events. See II Thessalonians 2:3-4 for the Abomination of Desolation.

2   (24:20) Israel today again observes its Sabbath day. With gas stations closed and many traffic lights off—in addition to some orthodox men physically retarding traffic—a mass evacuation in Jerusalem on the sabbath would be a bedlam situation.

3   (24:30) And I will pour upon the house of David, and upon the inhabitants of Jerusalem, the spirit of grace and of supplications: and they shall look upon Me whom they have pierced, and they shall mourn for Him, as one mourneth for his only son, and shall be in bitterness for Him, as one that is in bitterness for his firstborn (Zechariah 12:10).

PAST	PRESENT	RAPTURE	FIRST 3½	LAST 3½	ARMA-GEDDON	MIL-LENNIUM	NEW HEAVENS & EARTH
			TRIBULATION				

Petra, where many believe the Jews will seek safety when Antichrist begins his persecution in Jerusalem. Photo shows Diane Kirban on recent visit to this "Rose Red City" in Jordan. Scene is vast amphitheater built in 200 A.D. by the Romans. It is hewn out of living rock and has 34 tiers of seats that could seat some 3000 spectators. In the background are a few of the hundreds of caves.

(Matthew 24:21)

THE GREAT TRIBULATION

Some scholars reserve the title "Great Tribulation" for only the latter half of the 7 year Tribulation Period. During this latter 3-1/2 years the troubles of the Tribulation Period reach their zenith. This is sometimes called "The time of Jacob's trouble." (See Jeremiah 30:7 and Revelation 7:14).

That the Tribulation is composed of a 7 year period divided into 3-1/2 year halves can be seen from the following verses: Daniel 9:27; Revelation 11:2, 11:3, 12:6, 12:14, and 13:5.

Parable of Fig Tree
Mark 13:28-31
Luke 21:29-33

32 Now learn a parable of the fig tree: When its branch is yet tender, and putteth forth leaves, ye know that summer *is* near;

33 So likewise ye, when ye shall see all these things, know that it is near, *even* at the doors.

1 34 Verily I say unto you, This generation shall not pass, till all these things be fulfilled.

35 Heaven and earth shall pass away, but My words shall not pass away.

No Man Knows
the Hour of Christ's
Second Coming
Mark 13:32-37
Luke 21:34-36

2 36 But of that day and hour knoweth no *man,* no, not the angels of heaven, but My Father only.

37 But as the days of Noah *were,* so shall also the coming of the Son of man be.

38 For as in the days that were before the flood they were eating and drinking, marrying and giving in marriage, until the day that Noah entered into the ark,

39 And knew not until the flood came, and took them all away, so shall also the coming of the Son of man be.

40 Then shall two be in the field; the one shall be taken, and the other left.

41 Two *women shall be* grinding at the mill; the one shall be taken, and the other left.

42 Watch, therefore; for ye know not what hour your Lord doth come.

43 But know this, that if the householder had known in what watch the thief would come, he would have watched, and would not have allowed his house to be broken into.

44 Therefore be ye also ready; for in such an hour as ye think not the Son of man cometh.

45 Who, then, is a faithful and wise servant, whom his lord hath made ruler over his household, to give them food in due season?

46 Blessed *is* that servant, whom his lord, when he cometh, shall find so doing.

47 Verily I say unto you that he shall make him ruler over all his goods.

48 But and if that evil servant shall say in his heart, My lord delayeth his coming;

49 And shall begin to smite *his* fellow servants, and to eat and drink with the drunkards,

50 The lord of that servant shall come in a day when he looketh not for *him,* and in an hour that he is not aware of,

51 And shall cut him asunder, and 3 appoint *him* his portion with the hypocrites; there shall be weeping and gnashing of teeth.

CHAPTER 25

The Parable of The 10 Virgins
●Mt. of Olives

1 Then shall the kingdom of heaven 4 be likened unto ten virgins, who took their lamps, and went forth to meet the bridegroom.

2 And five of them were wise, and five *were* foolish.

3 They that *were* foolish took their lamps, and took no oil with them;

---

1 (24:34) Those alive at the start of the Tribulation unless killed, will see its end.

2 (24:36-51) Christ prophesies of the evil days which will precede both His Coming at the Rapture and the events which follow.

3 (24:51) Judgment at the Tribulation, at Armageddon, and at the Great White Throne. Revelation 20:11-15.

4 (25:1-30) Here Christ speaks of conduct in the present age preceding the events of the Rapture, Tribulation and Armageddon. Believers will be judged after the Rapture for rewards at the Judgment Seat of Christ (II Corinthians 5:10). Unbelievers will be judged by the Tribulation calamities and at the Judgment of those surviving Armageddon (verses 31-46), as well as at the final Great White Throne Judgment of Revelation 20:11-15.

4 But the wise took oil in their vessels with their lamps.

5 While the bridegroom tarried, they all slumbered and slept.

6 And at midnight there was a cry made, Behold, the bridegroom cometh; go ye out to meet him.

7 Then all those virgins arose and trimmed their lamps.

8 And the foolish said unto the wise, Give us of your oil; for our lamps are gone out.

9 But the wise answered, saying, *Not so,* lest there be not enough for us and you; but go rather to them that sell, and buy for yourselves.

10 And while they went to buy, the bridegroom came, and they that were ready went in with him to the marriage; and the door was shut.

11 Afterward came also the other virgins, saying, Lord, Lord, open to us.

12 But he answered and said, Verily I say unto you, I know you not.

13 Watch, therefore; for ye know neither the day nor the hour in which the Son of man cometh.

The Parable of The Talents (Money)

14 For *the kingdom of heaven is* like a man traveling into a far country, *who* called his own servants and delivered unto them his goods.

15 And unto one he gave five talents [$5,000], to another two [$2,000], and to another one [$1,000], to every man according to his ability; and straightway took his journey.

16 Then he that had received the five talents went and traded with the same, and made other five talents.

17 And likewise he that *had received* two, he also gained other two.

18 But he that had received one went and dug in the earth, and hid his lord's money.

19 After a long time the lord of those servants cometh, and reckoneth with them.

20 And so he that had received five talents came and brought other five talents [$10,000 total], saying, Lord, thou deliveredst unto me five talents; behold, I have gained beside them five talents more.

21 His lord said unto him, Well done, *thou* good and faithful servant; thou hast been faithful over a few things, I will make thee ruler over many things. Enter thou into the joy of thy lord.

22 He also that had received two talents came and said, Lord, thou deliveredst unto me two talents; behold, I have gained two other talents beside them.

23 His lord said unto him, Well done, good and faithful servant; thou hast been faithful over a few things, I will make thee ruler over many things. Enter thou into the joy of thy lord.

24 Then he that had received the one talent came and said, Lord, I knew thee, that thou art an hard man, reaping where thou hast not sown, and gathering where thou hast not spread,

25 And I was afraid, and went and hid thy talent in the earth; lo, *there* thou hast *what is* thine.

26 His lord answered and said unto him, *Thou* wicked and slothful servant, thou knewest that I reap where I sowed not, and gather where I have not spread?

27 Thou oughtest, therefore, to have put my money to the exchangers, and *then,* at my coming, I should have received mine own with interest.

28 Take, therefore, the talent from him, and give *it* unto him who hath ten talents [$10,000].

29 For unto every one that hath shall be given, and he shall have abundance; but from him that hath

1   (25:15) The approximate dollar equivalents have been supplied in brackets.

PAST	PRESENT	RAPTURE	FIRST 3½ LAST 3½ TRIBULATION		ARMA-GEDDON	MIL-LENNIUM	NEW HEAVENS & EARTH
			FIRST 3½	LAST 3½			

not shall be taken away even that which he hath.

30 And cast the unprofitable servant into outer darkness; there shall be weeping and gnashing of teeth.

Day of Judgment for Individual Gentiles When Christ Returns to Earth

1 31 When the Son of man shall come in His glory, and all the holy angels with Him, then shall He sit upon the throne of His glory.

32 And before Him shall be gathered all the nations; and He shall separate them one from another, as a shepherd divideth *His* sheep from the goats.

33 And He shall set the sheep on His right hand, but the goats on the left.

34 Then shall the King say unto them on His right hand, Come, ye blessed of My Father, inherit the kingdom prepared for you from the foundation of the world;

35 For I was hungry, and ye gave Me food; I was thirsty, and ye gave Me drink; I was a stranger, and ye took Me in;

36 Naked, and ye clothed Me; I was sick, and ye visited Me; I was in prison, and ye came unto Me.

37 Then shall the righteous answer Him, saying, Lord, when saw we thee hungry, and fed *thee;* or thirsty, and gave *thee* drink?

38 When saw we thee a stranger, and took *thee* in; or naked, and clothed *thee*?

39 Or when saw we thee sick, or in prison, and came unto thee?

40 And the King shall answer and say unto them, Verily I say unto you, Inasmuch as ye have done *it* unto one of the least of these My brethren, ye have done *it* unto Me.

41 Then shall He say also unto them on the left hand, Depart from Me, ye cursed, into everlasting fire, prepared for the devil and his angels;

42 For I was hungry, and ye gave Me no food; I was thirsty, and ye gave Me no drink;

43 I was a stranger, and ye took Me not in; naked, and ye clothed Me not; sick, and in prison, and ye visited Me not.

44 Then shall they also answer Him, saying, Lord, when saw we thee hungry, or athirst, or a stranger, or naked, or sick, or in prison, and did not minister unto thee?

45 Then shall He answer them, saying, Verily I say unto you, Inasmuch as ye did *it* not to one of the least of these, ye did *it* not to Me.

46 And these shall go away into everlasting punishment, but the righteous into life eternal.

CHAPTER 26

Chief Priests Conspire to Kill Christ

● *Mt. of Olives*
Mark 14:1-2
Luke 22:1-2

1 And it came to pass that, when Jesus had finished all these sayings, He said unto His disciples,

2 Ye know that after two days is *the feast of* the passover, and the Son of man is betrayed to be crucified.

3 Then assembled together the chief priests, and the scribes, and the elders of the people, unto the palace of the high priest, who was called Caiaphas,

4 And consulted that they might take Jesus by subtlety, and kill *Him*.

5 But they said, Not on the feast *day,* lest there be an uproar among the people.

---

1 (25:31-46) This is the judgment of those still alive immediately following Armageddon.

PAST	PRESENT	RAPTURE	FIRST 3½ LAST 3½ TRIBULATION		ARMA-GEDDON	MIL-LENNIUM	NEW HEAVENS & EARTH

Even a child has talents that can be used for the Lord. The songs of Christmas should be reflected in our walk every day of the year.

(Matthew 25:27)

THE UNPROFITABLE SERVANT

There are over 14,000 banks in the United States; 52 of which have deposits of over $1 Billion each! And how often do you read or hear of a Christian who accumulated wealth, failed to make a will, and thus his money was dissipated by taxes and squabbling relatives. This was not a wise use of money.

A talent, probably worth about $1000 in those days, represented a sizable amount of money. But this parable refers not only to money but also to the multiplying of one's time in the work of the Lord.

Regardless of whether one's financial or service abilities are singular (one talent) or multiple (5 talents) they must not be buried but rather put to use...productive use. As it is folly for a man to hide his money under a mattress when there are over 14,000 banks willing to pay interest...it is far more folly to be an unprofitable servant of God.

(Matthew 25:32)

JUDGMENTS and their DISTINCTION

There are 4 judgments in Scripture of which you should be aware:

1. Judgment of the Church ("The Judgment Seat of Christ")
   2 Corinthians 5:10-11

Here we have the judgment of the believer's works...not his sins. Hebrews 10:17 tells us that the Christian's sins and iniquities will be remembered no more. But Matthew 12:36, Romans 14:10, Colossians 3:24-25 remind us that every work must come to judgment. This judgment **occurs at the return of Christ for His church** (Rapture)...immediately after the Rapture but before the marriage supper of the Lamb.

2. Judgment of individual Gentiles
   Verse 32 of Matthew 25 refers to this.

This event is fully anticipated in the Old Testament. See Psalm 2:1-10, Isaiah 63:1-6, Joel 3:2-16; Zephaniah 3:8 and Zechariah 14:1-3.

Here the sheep (believers) are separated from the goats (unbelievers). This **occurs after the Tribulation Period** when those Gentiles who have come to Christ during this perilous period will be ushered into the kingdom and eternal life. The goats (unbelievers) will be cast into everlasting fire for their sins.

3. Judgment of Israel
   Ezekiel 20:33-38

When Christ returns **after the Tribulation Period** He will regather the Jews and purge those who rebelled. This will be accomplished after He first delivers the whole nation from its persecutors. Those who, like the sheep among the Gentiles, are believers in Jesus Christ will be ushered into the kingdom.

4. Judgment of the Wicked
   Revelation 20:11-15

For this judgment we look to the time **after the Millennium** (1000 years). This last judgment comes to all unbelievers of all ages at the Great White Throne. The Holy God, the Sovereign Judge, will be seated on the throne. These unbelievers will be judged according to their sinful works. And because not one of them has his name written in the Lamb's book of life...they will be cast into the lake of fire.

There will be no escape forever!

These stone steps could very well be the very same stones on which Jesus walked to be tried by Caiaphas (Matthew 26:57). This path is at the Palace of Caiaphas. Caiaphas was the high priest at the time of Jesus' arrest and crucifixion.

Mary of Bethany Annoints
Feet of Jesus
Saturday evening,
April, 30 A.D.
● *Bethany*
Mark 14:3-9
John 12:2-8

6 Now when Jesus was in Bethany, in the house of Simon, the leper,
7 There came unto Him a woman having an alabaster box of very precious ointment, and poured it on His head, as He *was eating.*
8 But when His disciples saw *it,* they had indignation, saying, To what purpose *is* this waste?
9 For this ointment might have been sold for much, and given to the poor.
10 When Jesus understood *it,* He said unto them, Why trouble ye the woman? For she hath wrought a good work upon Me.
11 For ye have the poor always with you, but Me ye have not always.
12 For in that she hath poured this ointment on My body, she did *it* for My burial.
13 Verily I say unto you, Wherever this gospel shall be preached in the whole world, *there* shall also this, that this woman hath done, be told for a memorial of her.

Judas Agrees to Betray Jesus
for About $20

14 Then one of the twelve, called Judas Iscariot, went unto the chief priests,
15 And said *unto them,* What will ye give me, and I will deliver Him unto you? And they bargained with him for thirty pieces of silver.
16 And from that time he sought opportunity to betray Him.

Preparation for the Passover
Thursday evening,
April, 30 A.D.
● *Jerusalem*
Mark 14:12-16
Luke 22:7-13

17 Now on the first *day* of the *feast* of unleavened bread, the disciples came to Jesus, saying unto Him, Where wilt thou that we prepare for thee to eat the passover?
18 And He said, Go into the city to such a man, and say unto him, The Master saith, My time is at hand; I will keep the passover at thy house with My disciples.
19 And the disciples did as Jesus had appointed them, and they made ready the passover.

The Last Passover
Judas Unmasked
● *Upper Room, Jerusalem*
Psalm 41:9
Mark 14:17-21
Luke 22:14-20

20 Now when the evening was come, He sat down with the twelve.
21 And as they did eat, He said, Verily I say unto you that one of you shall betray Me.
22 And they were exceedingly sorrowful, and began every one of them to say unto Him, Lord, is it I?
23 And He answered and said, He that dippeth *his* hand with Me in the dish, the same shall betray Me. [1]
24 The Son of man goeth as it is written of Him; but woe unto that man by whom the Son of man is betrayed! It had been good for that man if he had not been born.
25 Then Judas, who betrayed Him, answered and said, Master, is it I? He said unto him, Thou hast said.

---

1 (26:23) Yea, Mine own familiar friend, in whom I trusted, which did eat of My bread, hath lifted up his heel against Me (Psalm 41:9).

PAST	PRESENT	RAPTURE	FIRST 3½ LAST 3½ TRIBULATION		ARMA-GEDDON	MIL-LENNIUM	NEW HEAVENS & EARTH

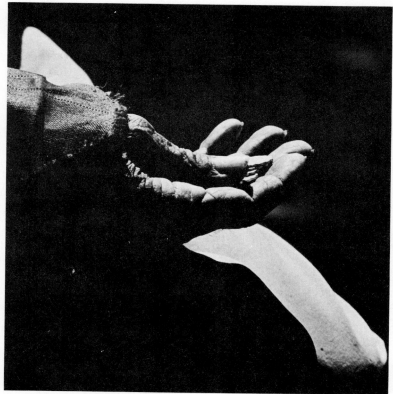

Are we more concerned with material gain selling our spiritual dedication for temporary riches?

(Matthew 26:15)

BETRAYED FOR ABOUT $20

In reading this account in verses 14 and 15 it is easy for us to look in scorn upon Judas for betraying Christ for a mere equivalent of $20.

And yet the mounting possessions of American families has risen dramatically just in the last 10 years. 10 years ago only 16.4% of Americans were 2 car families. Now, over 30% of American families have 2 cars.

Just 10 years ago only 5% of Americans had color television. Now over 40% have color television.

Could it possibly be, in one sense of the word, that we Christians betray Christ through our obsession with material possessions? Our 30 pieces of silver may be a $4000 automobile. And this lack of dedication on our part may in some measure be responsible for the lack of results on the mission fields both here at home and abroad.

The Lord's Supper Instituted
Mark 14:22-25
Luke 22:17-20

26 And as they were eating, Jesus took bread, and blessed *it,* and broke *it,* and gave *it* to the disciples, and said, Take, eat; this is My body.

27 And He took the cup, and gave thanks, and gave *it* to them, saying, Drink ye all of it;

28 For this is My blood of the new testament, which is shed for many for the remission of sins.

29 But I say unto you, I will not drink henceforth of this fruit of the vine, until that day when I drink it new with you in My Father's kingdom.

Peter's 3-Time Denial Foretold
● *Mt. of Olives*
Psalm 42:6
Zechariah 13:7
Mark 14:26-31
Luke 22:31-34
John 13:31-38

30 And when they had sung an hymn, they went out into the Mount of Olives.

1 31 Then saith Jesus unto them, All ye shall be offended because of Me this night; for it is written, I will smite the shepherd, and the sheep of the flock shall be scattered abroad.

2 32 But after I am raised up again, I will go before you into Galilee.

33 Peter answered and said unto Him, Though all *men* shall be offended because of thee, *yet* will I never be offended.

3 34 Jesus said unto him, Verily I say unto thee that this night, before the cock crows, thou shalt deny Me thrice.

35 Peter said unto Him, Though I should die with thee, yet will I not deny thee. Likewise also said all the disciples.

Jesus Prays in Gethsemane
● *Gethsemane*
Mark 14:32-42
Luke 22:39-46
John 18:1

36 Then cometh Jesus with them unto a place called Gethsemane, and saith unto the disciples, Sit here, while I go and pray yonder.

37 And He took with Him Peter and the two sons of Zebedee, and began to be sorrowful and very depressed.

38 Then saith He unto them, My soul is exceedingly sorrowful, even unto death; tarry here, and watch with Me.

The First Prayer
Mark 14:35
Luke 22:41-42

39 And He went a little further, and fell on His face, and prayed, saying, O My Father, if it be possible, let this cup pass from Me; nevertheless, not as I will, but as thou *wilt.*

The Disciples Sleep
Mark 14:37-40
Luke 22:45-46

40 And He cometh unto the disciples, and findeth them asleep; and He saith unto Peter, What, could ye not watch with Me one hour?

41 Watch and pray, that ye enter not into temptation; the spirit indeed *is* willing, but the flesh *is* weak.

---

1   (26:31) Awake, O sword, against My shepherd, and against the man that is My fellow, saith the Lord of hosts: smite the shepherd, and the sheep shall be scattered: and I will turn Mine hand upon the little ones (Zechariah 13:7).

2   (26:32) Matthew 28:7.

3   (26:34) Matthew 26:69-75.

PAST	PRESENT	RAPTURE	FIRST 3½ LAST 3½ TRIBULATION		ARMA-GEDDON	MIL-LENNIUM	NEW HEAVENS & EARTH

Garden of Gethsemane, the place of Jesus' agony and arrest (Matthew 26:36-56).

(Matthew 26:36)

IS ONE HOUR TOO MUCH TO ASK?

Gethsemane is where Jesus often went to pray (Luke 22:39). Judas seemed to know where he could find Jesus to betray Him. Here is where Christ agonized in those few remaining hours before His arrest.

And it was here that He bid Peter and the 2 sons of Zebedee to come and "...watch with Me" (verse 38). What happened? When Jesus returned He found them asleep! His haunting question was, "...could ye not watch with Me one hour?" (verse 40).

What a lesson for us? Christ in His greatest hour of agony found His own disciples asleep! How difficult is it for you to spend just one hour in the Lord's house on Sunday? And how often during this one hour is your mind wandering to events of the past week or plans for the coming week? In fact, could we not compare our brief sojourn on earth as our "one hour" which we are asked to spend loyal to Christ?

We cannot blame the disciples for their lack of devotion without also pointing the finger at our own life. If Christ is all in all, how much more of our time should we devote to His ministry!

The Second Prayer
Thursday, midnight
April, 30 A.D.
Mark 14:39
Luke 22:44

42 He went away again the second time, and prayed, saying, O My Father, if this cup may not pass away from Me except I drink it, thy will be done.

43 And He came and found them asleep again; for their eyes were heavy.

The Third Prayer
Mark 14:41

44 And He left them, and went away again, and prayed the third time, saying the same words.

45 Then cometh He to His disciples, and saith unto them, Sleep on now, and take *your* rest; behold, the hour is at hand, and the Son of man is betrayed into the hands of sinners.

46 Rise, let us be going; behold, he is at hand that doth betray Me.

Betrayal and
Arrest of Jesus
• *Gethsemane*
Mark 14:43-50
Luke 22:47-53
John 18:3-11

47 And while He yet spoke, lo, Judas, one of the twelve, came, and with him a great multitude with swords and clubs, from the chief priests and elders of the people.

1 48 Now he that betrayed Him gave them a sign, saying, Whomsoever I shall kiss, that same is He; hold Him fast.

49 And forthwith he came to Jesus, and said, Hail, Master; and kissed Him.

50 And Jesus said unto him, Friend, why art thou come? Then came they, and laid hands on Jesus, and took Him.

51 And, behold, one of those who were with Jesus stretched out *his* hand, and drew his sword, and struck a servant of the high priest's, and smote off his ear.

52 Then said Jesus unto him, Put up again thy sword into place; for all they that take the sword shall perish with the sword.

53 Thinkest thou that I cannot now pray to My Father, and He shall presently give Me more than twelve legions of angels?

54 But how, then, shall the scriptures be fulfilled, that thus it must be?   2

55 In that same hour said Jesus to the multitudes, Are ye come out as against a thief with swords and clubs to take Me? I sat daily with you teaching in the temple, and ye laid no hold on Me.

56 But all this was done, that the   3
scriptures of the prophets might be fulfilled. Then all the disciples forsook Him, and fled.

Christ Before Caiaphas
Last Day
Early Friday, April, 30 A.D.
• *Jerusalem*
Mark 14:53-65
John 18:24

57 And they that had laid hold on Jesus led *Him* away to Caiaphas, the high priest, where the scribes and the elders were assembled.

58 But Peter followed Him afar off unto the high priest's court, and went in, and sat with the guards, to see the end.

59 Now the chief priests, and elders, and all the council, sought false witness against Jesus, to put Him to death,

60 But found none; yea, though many false witnesses came, *yet* found they none. At the last came two false witnesses,

---

1   (26:48) Yea, Mine own familiar friend, in whom I trusted, which did eat of My bread, hath lifted up his heel against Me (Psalm 41:9).

2   (26:54) Isaiah 53; Psalm 22; Zechariah 13:7.

3   (26:56) ...And He was numbered with the transgressors (Isaiah 53:12).

1 61 And said, This *fellow* said, I am able to destroy the temple of God, and to build it in three days.

62 And the high priest arose and said unto Him, Answerest thou nothing? What *is it which* these witness against thee?

63 But Jesus held His peace. And the high priest answered and said unto Him, I adjure thee by the living God, that thou tell us whether thou be the Christ, the Son of God.

2 64 Jesus saith unto him, Thou hast said; nevertheless, I say unto you, Hereafter shall ye see the Son of man sitting on the right hand of power, and coming in the clouds of heaven.

65 Then the high priest tore his clothes, saying, He hath spoken blasphemy! What further need have we of witnesses? Behold, now ye have heard His blasphemy.

66 What think ye? They answered and said, He is guilty of death.

67 Then they spat in His face, and buffeted Him; and others smote *Him* with the palms of their hands,

68 Saying, Prophesy unto us, thou Christ, Who smote thee?

Peter Denies Christ 3 Times
Mark 14:66-72
Luke 22:55-62
John 18:15-18, 25-27

69 Now Peter sat outside in the court, and a maid came unto him, saying, Thou also wast with Jesus of Galilee.

70 But he denied *it* before *them* all, saying, I know not what thou sayest.

71 And when he was gone out into the porch, another *maid* saw him, and said unto them that were there, This *fellow* was also with Jesus of Nazareth.

72 And again he denied with an oath, I do not know the man.

73 And after a while came unto *him* they that stood by, and said to Peter, Surely thou also art *one* of them; for thy speech betrayeth thee.

74 Then began he to curse and to 3 swear, *saying,* I know not the man. And immediately the cock crowed.

75 And Peter remembered the word of Jesus, who said unto him, Before the cock crows, thou shalt deny Me thrice. And he went out, and wept bitterly.

CHAPTER 27

Jesus Taken to Pilate
● *Jerusalem*
Psalm 110:1
Mark 15:1
Luke 23:1
John 18:28

1 When the morning was come, all the chief priests and elders of the people took counsel against Jesus to put Him to death:

2 And when they had bound Him, they led *Him* away, and delivered Him to Pontius Pilate, the governor.

---

1 (26:61) John 2:19-22.

2 (26:64) I saw in the night visions, and, behold, one like the Son of man came with clouds of heaven, and came to the Ancient of days, and they brought Him near before Him.

   And there was given Him dominion, and glory, and a kingdom, that all people, nations, and languages, should serve Him: His dominion is an everlasting dominion, which shall not pass away, and His kingdom that which shall not be destroyed (Daniel 7:13-14).

3 (26:74-75) Matthew 26:34.

PAST	PRESENT	RAPTURE	FIRST 3½ LAST 3½ TRIBULATION		ARMA- GEDDON	MIL- LENNIUM	NEW HEAVENS & EARTH

(Matthew 26:50)

THE COMPASSIONATE JESUS

Look at the picture in verse 50. Imagine in your mind's eye Jesus alone praying in the Garden of Gethsemane in the stillness of the night. Suddenly a great multitude of men come with swords and clubs led by Judas...the apostle.

How did Jesus react? Look at verse 50. His approach and question began with the word "Friend...." In spite of Judas' betrayal Christ was still reaching out to Judas in friendship. Right there Judas could have repented and he would have been forgiven. What a picture of the compassionate Jesus!

No doubt the Romans did not bring for the arrest a full legion of men... but exactly how many soldiers they brought we do not know. A legion in Roman days was about 6000 men. Jesus in verse 53 reminded them he could call on 12 legions of angels (72,000)...but to do so would not be in fulfillment of God's sovereign plan (Matthew 26:53-54).

A Czechoslovakian woman cries in anguish as she holds photo of her country's deposed leader in defiance of invading Russian troops. Are today's Christians lax in their testimony because they take freedom for granted?

Judas Hangs Himself
Acts 1:18-19

1　3 Then Judas, who had betrayed Him, when he saw that He was condemned, repented, and brought again the thirty pieces of silver to the chief priests and elders,
4 Saying, I have sinned in that I have betrayed innocent blood. And they said, What *is that* to us? See thou *to that.*
5 And he cast down the pieces of silver in the temple, and departed, and went and hanged himself.

Friday forenoon,
April, 30 A.D.

6 And the chief priests took the silver pieces, and said, It is not lawful to put them into the treasury, because it is the price of blood.
7 And they took counsel, and bought with them the potter's field, to bury strangers in.
8 Wherefore, that field was called, The field of blood, unto this day.
9 Then was fulfilled that which was spoken by Jeremiah, the prophet, saying, And they took the thirty pieces of silver, the price of Him that was valued, whom they of the children of Israel did value.
10 And gave them for the potter's field, as the Lord appointed me.

First Appearance Before Pilate
Mark 15:2-5
Luke 23:2-3
John 18:29-38

11 And Jesus stood before the governor; and the governor asked Him, saying, Art thou the King of the Jews? And Jesus said unto him, Thou sayest.

12 And when He was accused by　2 the chief priests and elders, He answered nothing.
13 Then said Pilate unto Him, Hearest thou not how many things they witness against thee?
14 And He answered him never a word, insomuch that the governor marveled greatly.

Second Appearance
Before Pilate
Mark 15:6-15
Luke 23:13-25
John 18:39-19:16

15 Now at *that* feast the governor was accustomed to releasing unto the people a prisoner, whom they would.
16 And they had then a notable prisoner, called Barabbas.
17 Therefore, when they were gathered together, Pilate said unto them, Whom will ye that I release unto you? Barabbas, or Jesus, who is called Christ?
18 For he knew that for envy they had delivered Him.
19 When he was seated on the judgment seat, his wife sent unto him, saying, Have thou nothing to do with that righteous man; for I have suffered many things this day in a dream because of Him.
20 But the chief priests and elders persuaded the multitude that they should ask *for* Barabbas, and destroy Jesus.

Jesus or Barabbas

21 The governor answered and said unto them, Which of the two will ye that I release unto you? They said, Barabbas.

1　(27:3-10) Zechariah 11:12-13 in mystery-form foretold this. The connecting of Jeremiah's name, to this prophecy, verse 9, may be due to Jeremiah's having given the prophecy earlier, and then Zechariah later putting it in writing. Early Greek New Testament manuscripts used abbreviations for names. Jeremiah was *Iriou*, and Zechariah was *Zriou*. The two differ by only the direction of the central stroke of the first letter. Simeon suggested that here Matthew wrote *Zriou* but a latter scribe quickly copied it as *Iriou*.

2　(27:12) He was oppressed, and He was afflicted, yet He opened not His mouth: He is brought as a lamb to the slaughter, and as a sheep before her shearers is dumb, so He openeth not His mouth (Isaiah 53:7).

22 Pilate saith unto them, What shall I do then with Jesus, who is called Christ? *They* all say unto him, Let Him be crucified.

23 And the governor said, Why, what evil hath He done? But they cried out the more, saying, Let Him be crucified.

24 When Pilate saw that he could prevail nothing, but *that* rather a tumult was made, he took water, and washed *his* hands before the multitude, saying, I am innocent of the blood of this righteous person. See ye *to it.*

25 Then answered all the people, and said, His blood *be* on us, and on our children.

26 Then released he Barabbas unto them; and when he had scourged Jesus, he delivered *Him* to be crucified.

Christ Mocked by Soldiers
Mark 15:16-19

27 Then the soldiers of the governor took Jesus into the common hall, and gathered unto Him the whole band *of soldiers.*

28 And they stripped Him, and put on Him a scarlet robe.

1 29 And when they had plaited a crown of thorns, they put *it* upon His head, and a reed in His right hand; and they bowed the knee before Him, and mocked Him, saying, Hail, King of the Jews!

2 30 And they spat upon Him, and took the reed, and smote Him on the head.

Christ Led to Golgotha
Psalm 69:21
Mark 15:20-23
Luke 23:26-33
John 19:16-17

3 31 And after they had mocked Him, they took the robe off from Him, and put His own raiment on Him, and led Him away to crucify *Him.*

32 And as they came out, they found a man of Cyrene, Simon by name; him they compelled to bear His cross.

33 And when they were come unto a place called Golgotha, that is to say, a place of a skull,

4 34 They gave Him vinegar to drink, mingled with gall; and when He had tasted *it,* He would not drink.

Jesus Crucified
First 3 Hours on Cross

● *Calvary*
Psalm 22:18
Mark 15:24-32
Luke 23:33-43
John 19:18-27

5 35 And they crucified Him, and parted His garments, casting lots, that it might be fulfilled which was spoken by the prophet, They parted My garments among them, and upon My vesture did they cast lots.

36 And sitting down they watched Him there,

37 And set up over His head His accusation written, THIS IS JESUS, THE KING OF THE JEWS.

---

1 (27:29) As many were astonied at thee; His visage was so marred more than any man, and His form more than the sons of men (Isaiah 52:14).

2 (27:30) He is despised and rejected of men; a man of sorrows, and acquainted with grief: and we hid as it were our faces from Him; He was despised, and we esteemed Him not (Isaiah 53:3).

3 (27:31) He was taken from prison and from judgment: and who shall declare His generation? (Isaiah 53:8).

4 (27:34) They gave Me also gall for My meat; and in My thirst they gave Me vinegar to drink (Psalm 69:21).

5 (27:35) They part My garments among them, and cast lots upon My vesture (Psalm 22:18).

PAST	PRESENT	RAPTURE	FIRST 3½ LAST 3½ TRIBULATION		ARMA-GEDDON	MIL-LENNIUM	NEW HEAVENS & EARTH

Failure to follow the Lord always ends in tragedy. "There is a way which seemeth right unto a man but the end thereof are the ways of death" (Proverbs 14:12). Judas found this out. When Saul, faced with a superior enemy and the discouragement of his own army, acted on his own...it led to Endor. This illustration shows Samuel appearing, having been called by the witch of Endor (now called a medium). Saul had previously sinned in deliberate disobedience when he spared Agag and the best of the cattle God had told him to destroy. See 1 Samuel 15:9

(Matthew 27:7)

THE FIELD OF BLOOD

Potter's Field in Jerusalem has often been referred to as the Field of Blood (verse 8). Acts 1:19 preserves for us the Hebrew name, **Aceldama,** which comes from **aceld,** field, and **dama,** blood.

It is located on the southern side of the Valley of Hinnom, where it meets the Kidron Valley at the foot of the hill. It was purchased by the high priests with the 30 pieces of silver Judas threw down in the Temple after he realized the extent of his crime of betraying Jesus. See Matthew 27:3-10.

(Matthew 27:21)
THE CHOICE

Christ was condemned under 2 legal systems.

1. The Jewish system
   This involved the arrest and proceedings under Annas, Caiaphas, and the Sanhedrin. These were under Jewish law. Annas was the former High Priest, and the father-in-law of Caiaphas, the High Priest at the time of Christ's trial.
   This trial was illegal because:
   - (A) The judges took part in the arrest...they were thus hostile and biased.
   - (B) There was no formal accusation.
   - (C) Trials of a criminal nature had to be started and conducted only during daylight hours.
   - (D) They sought admissions from Christ although according to law no accused could be convicted on his own evidence.

2. The Roman system
   These proceedings were under Pilate, the Roman Governor, and Herod Antipas, the Tetrarch of Galilee and Peraea. Pilate tried to push off the odium of the trial on Herod since Herod was in Jerusalem on that day and since Jesus was a Galilean.

   Pilate's actions after declaring Christ innocent (verse 24) were in direct contradiction to existing Roman law.

1 38 Then were there two thieves crucified with Him, one on the right hand, and another on the left.

2 39 And they that passed by reviled Him, wagging their heads,

40 And saying, Thou that destroyest the temple, and buildest *it* in three days, save thyself. If thou be the Son of God, come down from the cross.

41 Likewise also the chief priests, mocking *Him,* with the scribes and elders, said,

42 He saved others; Himself He cannot save. If He be the King of Israel, let Him now come down from the cross, and we will believe Him.

43 He trusted in God; let Him deliver Him now, if He will have Him; for He said, I am the Son of God.

44 The thieves also, who were crucified with Him, cast the same in His teeth.

Last 3 Hours on Cross
Friday afternoon,
April, 30 A.D.
Psalm 22:1
Mark 15:33-37
Luke 23:44-46
John 19:28-30

45 Now from the sixth hour there was darkness over all the land unto the ninth hour.

3 46 And about the ninth hour Jesus cried with a loud voice, saying, Eli, Eli, lama sabachthani? that is to say, My God, My God, why hast thou forsaken Me?

47 Some of them that stood there, when they heard *that,* said, This *man* calleth for Elijah.

48 And straightway one of them ran, and took a sponge, and filled *it* with vinegar, and put *it* on a reed, and gave Him to drink.

49 The rest said, Let be; let us see whether Elijah will come to save Him.

The Dispensation of Law Ends at Christ's Death

50 Jesus, when He had cried again with a loud voice, yielded up the spirit.

51 And, behold, the veil of the temple was torn in two from the top to the bottom; and the earth did quake, and the rocks were split;

52 And the graves were opened; and many bodies of the saints that slept were raised,

53 And came out of the graves after His resurrection, and went into the holy city, and appeared unto many.

54 Now, when the centurion, and they that were with him watching Jesus, saw the earthquake, and those things that were done, they feared greatly, saying, Truly, this was the Son of God.

---

1 (27:38) And He made His grave with the wicked, and with the rich in His death; because He had done no violence, neither was any deceit in His mouth.

Therefore will I divide Him a portion with the great, and He shall divide the spoil with the strong; because He hath poured out His soul unto death: and He was numbered with the transgressors and He bore the sin of many, and made intercession for the transgressors (Isaiah 53:9,12).

2 (27:39-44) But I am a worm, and no man; a reproach of men, and despised of the people.

All they that see Me laugh Me to scorn: they shoot out the lip, they shake the head, saying,

He trusted on the Lord that He would deliver Him: let Him deliver Him, seeing He delighted in Him (Psalm 22:6-8).

3 (27:46) My God, My God, why hast thou forsaken Me? Why are thou so far from helping Me, and from the words of My roaring? (Psalm 22:1). With this quotation of the words of Psalm 22 Christ identifies Himself with the Suffering Servant, the Messiah, of that psalm. Psalm 22, written 1000 years before Christ, has been well described as the Saviour's meditation from the cross. Read it with this in mind.

55 And many women were there beholding afar off, who followed Jesus from Galilee, ministering unto Him,

56 Among whom were Mary Magdalene, and Mary, the mother of James and Joses, and the mother of Zebedee's children.

Burial of Jesus
Burial between 3 and 6 p.m.
Friday, April, 30 A.D.
● *Jerusalem*
Mark 15:42-46
Luke 23:50-54
John 19:31-42

1 57 When the evening was come, there came a rich man of Arimathaea, named Joseph, who also himself was Jesus' disciple:

58 He went to Pilate, and begged the body of Jesus. Then Pilate commanded the body to be delivered.

59 And when Joseph had taken the body, he wrapped it in a clean linen cloth.

60 And laid it in his own new tomb, which he had hewn out in the rock; and he rolled a great stone to the door of the sepulcher, and departed.

Tomb Sealed and Guarded
Saturday, April, 30 A.D.
Mark 15:47
Luke 23:55-56

61 And there were Mary Magdalene, and the other Mary, sitting over against the sepulcher.

62 Now the next day, that followed the day of the preparation, the chief priests and Pharisees came together unto Pilate,

63 Saying, Sir, we remember that that deceiver said, while He was yet alive, After three days I will rise again. 2

64 Command, therefore, that the sepulcher be made sure until the third day, lest His disciples come by night, and steal Him away, and say unto the people, He is risen from the dead; so the last error shall be worse than the first.

65 Pilate said unto them, Ye have a watch; go your way, make *it* as sure as ye can.

66 So they went, and made the sepulcher sure, sealing the stone, and setting a watch.

CHAPTER 28

Women Visit Tomb
Christ's Resurrection
Sunday morning, April, 30 A.D.
● *Jerusalem*
Mark 16:1-8
Luke 24:1-11

1 In the end of the sabbath, as it began to dawn toward the first *day* of the week, came Mary Magdalene and the other Mary to see the sepulcher.

2 And, behold, there was a great earthquake; for an angel of the Lord descended from heaven, and came and rolled back the stone from the door, and sat upon it.

3 His countenance was like lightning, and his raiment white as snow;

---

1 (27:57, 60) And He made His grave with the wicked, and with the rich in His death; because He had done no violence, neither was any deceit in His mouth.

Therefore will I divide Him a portion with the great, and He shall divide the spoil with the strong; because He hath poured out His soul unto death: and He was numbered with the transgressors; and He bore the sin of many, and made intercession for the transgressors (Isaiah 53:9,12).

2 (27:63) John 2:19.

PAST	PRESENT	RAPTURE	FIRST 3½ LAST 3½ TRIBULATION		ARMA- GEDDON	MIL- LENNIUM	NEW HEAVENS & EARTH
			FIRST 3½	LAST 3½			

4 And for fear of him the keepers did shake, and became as dead *men.*

5 And the angel answered and said unto the women, Fear not; for I know that ye seek Jesus, who was crucified.

1 6 He is not here; for He is risen, as He said. Come, see the place where the Lord lay.

2 7 And go quickly, and tell His disciples that He is risen from the dead; and, behold, He goeth before you into Galilee. There shall ye see Him; lo, I have told you.

8 And they departed quickly from the sepulcher with fear and great joy, and did run to bring His disciples word.

9 And as they went to tell His disciples, behold, Jesus met them, saying, All hail. And they came and held Him by the feet, and worshiped Him.

3 10 Then said Jesus unto them, Be not afraid; go tell My brethren that they go into Galilee, and there shall they see Me.

Soldiers Bribed

11 Now when they were going, behold, some of the watch came into the city, and showed unto the chief priests all the things that were done.

12 And when they were assembled with the elders, and had taken

counsel, they gave much money unto the soldiers.

13 Saying, Say ye, His disciples came by night, and stole Him *away* while we slept.

14 And if this come to the governor's ears, we will persuade him, and secure you.

15 So they took the money, and did as they were taught; and this saying is commonly reported among the Jews until this day.

Appearance of Jesus to 500
● *Mountain in Galilee*   4

16 Then the eleven disciples went away into Galilee, into a mountain where Jesus had appointed them.

17 And when they saw Him, they worshiped Him; but some doubted.

18 And Jesus came and spoke unto them, saying, All authority is given unto Me in heaven and in earth.

The Great Commission
Mark 16:15-18
Luke 24:44-49

19 Go ye, therefore, and teach all 5 nations, baptizing them in the name of the Father, and of the Son, and of the Holy Spirit,

20 Teaching them to observe all things whatsoever I have commanded you; and, lo, I am with you always, *even* unto the end of the age. Amen.

---

1 (28:6) Isaiah 51:13 - 53:10a prophesies Christ's death for our sins, but Isaiah 53:10b-12 foretells His resurrection from the dead. Likewise Psalm 22:1-21 prophesies of the crucifixion, while Psalm 22:22-31 sees the resurrection. So, too, Psalm 16:10 forsees the Messiah's rising from the dead.

2 (28:7) Matthew 26:32.

3 (28:10) Matthew 26:32.

4 (28:16-17) Nevertheless the dimness shall not be such as was in her vexation, when at the first He lightly afflicted the land of Zebulun and the land of Naphtali, and afterward did more grievously afflict her by the way of the sea, beyond Jordan, in Galilee of the nations.

The people that walked in darkness have seen a great light: they that dwell in the land of the shadow of death, upon them hath the light shined (Isaiah 9:1-2).

5 (28:19) II Corinthians 13:14.

PAST	PRESENT	RAPTURE	FIRST 3½ LAST 3½ TRIBULATION	ARMA-GEDDON	MIL-LENNIUM	NEW HEAVENS & EARTH

THE GARDEN TOMB

It is believed by many that the Garden Tomb pictured above (sometimes called Gordon's Garden Tomb, because he discovered and identified it) is the actual tomb where Christ was buried and arose on the third day. This is located just outside of the old walled inner city of Jerusalem and is next to the hill called, "Gordon's Calvary."

THE FINAL ALIGNMENT OF NATIONS

At the end of Gentile world power, during the Tribulation Period, there will be **three** kingdoms and federations of nations who contest the authority of the 10 Federated States of Europe.

1. **The Northern confederacy**
   [Ezekiel 38:1-39:25 (esp. 38:15; 39:2); Daniel 11:40; Joel 2:1-27 (esp. 2:20); Isaiah 10:12; 30:31-33; 31:8-9]

   You will find the principal passage describing this northern confederacy in Ezekiel 38:2-6.

   Basically, here are the nations in the **northern** confederacy of Ezekiel 38:
   A. Gog, Meshech, and Tubal (vs. 2) - Russia.
   B. Persia (vs. 5) - Iran and Iraq.
   C. Ethiopia and Libya (vs. 5) - Northeast Africa.
   D. Gomer (vs. 6) - Germany (possibly East Germany).
   E. Togarmah (vs. 6) - Exact location uncertain, but in the Europe, Turkey, Syria crescent.

2. **The Asiatic confederacy**
   In Revelation 16:12 we read that Palestine, which will have become the center of the activity of Antichrist and his European federation...will be invaded by a great army coming from beyond the Euphrates known as the forces of "the kings of the east."

   This is the second great alliance of powers that threatens the authority of the Federated States of Europe and Antichrist. The nations will most likely include: China, Japan, Vietnam, Thailand and other Asian countries.

3. **The Arab confederacy**
   In Daniel 11:40 we find a third power in conflict with the European Federation of States. This is known as the King of the South. This power advances on Palestine and sets off a movement of nations that brings about its destruction. It would appear that the King of the South is Egypt aligned with other Arab nations and together allied with Russia (King of the North).

The above three alliances will challenge the ever growing power of Antichrist. Antichrist will be head of the 10 nation United States of EUROPE. This federation of states will probably include France, England, possibly West Germany and other Common Market countries and perhaps the Eastern European states now subservient to Russia. Perhaps even the United States will join this coalition of nations.

The prophecy is revealed in Revelation 17:12-13, which shows that these nations that were once a part of the Roman Empire will gather together and are going to enter into an agreement to give their authority to one man as their head (Daniel 7:7-8, 23-26 Cp. Revelation 13).

This one man will be the Antichrist!

Thus in the Tribulation Period we will find 4 great kingdoms as follows:
1. Russia and her allies (The Northern confederacy)
2. China and her allies (The Asiatic confederacy)
3. Egypt and her allies (The Arab confederacy)
4. United States of Europe (The 10 nation confederacy)

RUSSIA INVADES ISRAEL

The invasion of Palestine by Russia and her allies (The Northern confederacy) will bring Antichrist and his armies to the defense of Israel as her would-be protector.

Daniel 11:40-45 describes this invasion.

The following is a suggested order of events:

1. The campaign begins when Egypt and her allies (The Arab confederacy), move against the United States of Europe and Antichrist.
2. The Arab confederacy is joined by Russia and her allies (The Northern confederacy). Together they attack Antichrist's headquarters (Jerusalem) coming by land and sea.
3. Jerusalem is destroyed as a result of this attack (Zechariah 12:2). But the armies of The Northern confederacy are also destroyed (Ezekiel 39; Zechariah 12:4).
4. The full armies of Antichrist move into Palestine (Daniel 11:41) and conquer all that territory (Daniel 11:41-42). However Edom, Moab and Ammon will escape the tyrannical rule of Antichrist (Daniel 11:41). These areas are now in present day Jordan, and Petra is in the Edom section of Jordan.

Antichrist, under the great coalition of western nations (United States of Europe) will set up his headquarters in Jerusalem at the close of the Tribulation Period and reign over Israel. But not only will he reign over Israel and Europe but will also control the entire world.

China and her allies (The Asiatic confederacy) will march with 200 million men towards Jerusalem to contest the right of the United States of Europe to have world-wide dominion.

However, Antichrist, alarmed, decides to fight them on a battleground which will be to his advantage...the mountains of Judea (Mt. Megiddo).

When Antichrist with his western confederacy prepare to battle the Asiatic confederacy — suddenly the heavens open and the two opposing sides realize that some unusual occurrence is taking place directed by God. It is at this time they unite forces in order to devote all their energies into fighting the Lord Jesus Christ.

The battle at Armageddon is quickly over and Antichrist and the False Prophet are thrown into the Lake of Fire. The entire army is killed (Revelation 16:12-21; 19:11-21).

THE Coming SEQUENCE of EVENTS in
God's Prophetic Timetable

As far as leading Bible believing scholars can understand the scriptures—here are the future events **in the sequence they will occur.**

The **next** coming event on God's Timetable of prophecy is the **RAPTURE.** The word **Rapture** (to be "caught up") does not appear in the Bible. However it is used to describe the event of 1 Thessalonians 4:14-17 in which believers are "caught up" to be with Christ at His Second Coming.

In 1 Thessalonians 4:14-17 God's Word tells us:
> For the Lord Himself
> shall descend from Heaven with a shout...
> and the dead in Christ shall rise first:
> Then we which are alive and remain
> shall be caught up (RAPTURED)
> together with them in the clouds,
> to meet the Lord in the air:
> and so shall we ever be with the Lord.

RAPTURE refers to the time, prior to the start of the 7 year Tribulation Period, when believing Christians (both dead and alive) will "in the twinkling of an eye" rise up to meet Christ in the air.

Thus the SEQUENCE OF COMING EVENTS, according to God's Word appears to be as follows:

RAPTURE, including the FIRST RESURRECTION
    (This can occur at any time.) At Christ's appearing the dead in Christ shall also rise (1 Thessalonians 4 and Revelation 20).

TRIBULATION
    This will be a 7 year period, following the Rapture, of phenomenal world trial and suffering. It is at this time that Antichrist will reign over a federation of 10 nations which quite possibly can include the United States. See Daniel 9:27; Matthew 24:21.

JUDGMENT SEAT OF CHRIST
    Here the believers raptured into heaven will stand before their Lord to receive crowns and rewards. Their sins have already been paid for at the cross (2 Corinthians 5:10).

BATTLE OF ARMAGEDDON
    This will occur at the end of the 7 year Tribulation Period when the Lord Jesus Christ comes down from Heaven and wipes out the combined armies of more than 200 million men. The blood bath covers over 185 miles of Israel (See Revelation 14:20).

JUDGMENT OF THE NATIONS

After Armageddon Christ will personally inaugurate upon the earth His earthly Kingdom Reign. The people from all nations who have survived the Tribulation will be judged individually as to whether or not they may enter Christ's Kingdom (Matthew 25:31-46).

At this time the surviving unsaved, non-believers are judged before God, and the wicked are expelled from off the earth into hell, where they will await the final Judgment Day (Revelation 20:11-15).

The righteous, however, with joy will be permitted to enter the promised Millennial kingdom.

RESURRECTION of the TRIBULATION SAINTS

Those who have accepted Christ during the Tribulation will be raised from the dead by the close of the Tribulation's 7 years as part of the First Resurrection (Daniel 12:1-2 and Revelation 20).

DISPOSITION OF EVIL ONES

During this same time period...Antichrist and the False Prophet are thrown into the Lake of Fire (Revelation 19:20).

Satan is bound in the bottomless pit for 1000 years (Revelation 20:1-3).

MILLENNIAL ("1000 Years") REIGN OF CHRIST

When all the believers of all the ages reign with Christ. Christ will reign on this earth and Old Testament promised Kingdom prophecies of world peace will at last come true (See Isaiah 11 and Revelation 20).

THE FINAL REBELLION

At the end of the Millennium Satan will have a brief and last opportunity to deceive people. You must remember that many will be born during the Millennial period. Millions will follow Satan. This horde of perhaps millions of people will completely encircle the Believers and encompass Jerusalem in a state of siege.

When this occurs, God brings fire down from Heaven killing the millions of Satan's army (Revelation 20).

GREAT WHITE THRONE JUDGMENT

At this time the surviving unsaved, non-believers are judged before God, and the wicked are expelled from off the earth into hell, where they will await the final Judgment Day (Revelation 20:11-15). The righteous, however, with joy will be permitted to enter the promised millennial kingdom.

EARTH BURNS UP

To purify this earth God sets it afire with a fervent heat. See 2 Peter 3:7, 10.

The NEW HEAVEN and the NEW EARTH

All Christians finally reach the ultimate in glory reigning forever with Christ in a new heaven and a new, purged earth (Revelation 21).

This briefly covers the sequence of events. For a more thorough presentation we suggest you read GUIDE TO SURVIVAL and YOUR LAST GOODBYE...both by Salem Kirban.

THE APOSTLES...THEIR OCCUPATION, MINISTRY and END

Apostle	Original Occupation	Area of Ministry	How they Died
Peter	Fisherman	First leader of Christian church (Acts 1-15; Galatians 2:9)	*Crucified upside down at Rome (cf. John 21:18-19)
James (of Zebedee)	Fisherman	Preached in Judea	Beheaded by Herod Antipas c. 44 A.D. (Acts 12:1-2)
John (of Zebedee)	Fisherman	Jerusalem and Ephesus. Banished to Patmos.	Died natural death at Ephesus (John 21:20-23)
Andrew	Fisherman	Scythia, Greece, Asia Minor	*Crucified on a St. Andrew's Cross
Philip	Unknown	Phrygia	Died a martyr at Hierapolis, Turkey
Bartholomew	Unknown	Armenia (now in Turkey & Iran)	*Was flayed to death
Thomas	Unknown	Parthia, Persia and India	*Suffered martyrdom near Madras, India
Matthew	Tax Collector	Ethiopia	*Martyred
James the Less (Mark 3:14,18)	Unknown	Palestine and Egypt	*Crucified in Egypt
Jude	Unknown	Assyria and Persia (Iran)	*Martyred
Simon the Zealot	Unknown	Unknown	*Crucified
Judas Iscariot	Unknown	No known ministry	Hanged himself (Matthew 26:14-16)

*Exact way of death not known but based largely on tradition and historical writings. If these traditions have any truth in them, only one of the Apostles died a natural death; one committed suicide; and 10 suffered martyrdom, 4 of them by crucifixion.